TRIVShOT

1001

TRIVIA QUESTIONS

TOTTENHAM

HOTSPUR

FASCINATING FACTS! TRIVIA BRAINTEASERS!
WRITTEN AND ILLUSTRATED BY

DESIGNED BY JOE McGARRY

First published by Pitch Publishing, 2021

Pitch Publishing
A2 Yeoman Gate
Yeoman Way
Worthing
Sussex
BN13 3QZ
www.pitchpublishing.co.uk
info@pitchpublishing.co.uk

ISBN: 978 1 80150 014 2

Typesetting and origination by Pitch Publishing
Printed and bound in India by Replika Press Pvt. Ltd.

1001 TRIVIA QUESTIONS: TOTTENHAM HOTSPUR

Other books in this series:

**1001 TRIVIA QUESTIONS: ARSENAL
1001 TRIVIA QUESTIONS: MANCHESTER CITY
1001 TRIVIA QUESTIONS: MANCHESTER UNITED
1001 TRIVIA QUESTIONS: NEWCASTLE UNITED
1001 TRIVIA QUESTIONS: WEST HAM UNITED
1001 TRIVIA QUESTIONS: THIS DAY IN WORLD FOOTBALL**

ACKNOWLEDGEMENTS

Thanks to Joe McGarry for his brilliant design work and his technical expertise. There would be no books without him!

Thanks to Debs McGarry for the research and art assistance.

Thanks to Luke McGarry for picking up the slack on the other features while we worked on this.

Thanks to all three for their patience!

Additional thanks to Tom and Andy at "Shoot! The Breeze" podcast and Rob Stokes for the additional research and scans!

ABOUT STEVE McGARRY

A former record sleeve designer, whose clients included Joy Division, Steve McGarry is one of the most prolific and widely-published cartoonists and illustrators that Britain has ever produced. In the UK alone, his national newspaper daily strips include "Badlands", which ran for a dozen years in The Sun, "The Diary of Rock & Pop" in the Daily Star, "Pop Culture" in Today and "World Soccer Diary" in The Sun.

Over his four-decade career he has regularly graced the pages of soccer magazines Match, Match of the Day and Shoot! and his comics work ranges from Romeo in the 1970s and Look-In, Tiger and Oink! in the 1980s, SI for Kids and FHM in the 1990s, through to the likes of Viz, MAD and Toxic! When The People launched his Steve McGarry's 20th Century Heroes series, they billed him as the world's top cartoonist.

His sports features have been published worldwide since 1982 and he currently has two features – "Biographic" and "Kid Town" – in newspaper syndication, with a client list that includes the New York Daily News and The Washington Post.

In recent years, he has also created story art for such movies as "Despicable Me 2", "The Minions" and "The Secret Life of Pets".

Although Manchester born and bred, Steve has been based in California since 1989. A two-term former President of the National Cartoonists Society, his honours include Illustrator of the Year awards from the NCS and the Australian Cartoonists Association, and he is a recipient of the prestigious Silver T-Square for "outstanding service to the profession of cartooning". In 2013, he was elected President of the NCS Foundation, the charitable arm of the National Cartoonists Society. He is also the founder and director of US comics festival NCSFest.

1001 QUESTIONS

PORTUGEEZERS!

A GOALKEEPER WHO SPENT MUCH OF HIS CAREER AS A BACK-UP, **NUNO ESPÍRITO SANTO** WON MULTIPLE HONOURS WITH **PORTO** AND PLAYED FOR CLUBS IN SPAIN AND RUSSIA, HE LAUNCHED HIS MANAGEMENT CAREER WITH PORTUGAL'S **RIO AVE**, HAD SPELLS IN CHARGE OF **VALENCIA** AND **PORTO**, AND THEN FOUND SUCCESS WITH **WOLVERHAMPTON WANDERERS**, STEERING THE CLUB BACK TO THE TOP FLIGHT AS CHAMPIONS IN 2018. HE WAS APPOINTED **TOTTENHAM HOTSPUR** MANAGER THREE YEARS LATER.

IDENTIFY THESE OTHER PORTUGUESE CONNECTIONS TO **SPURS**:

1   WHICH **ENGLAND** DEFENDER GREW UP IN PORTUGAL AND BEGAN HIS CAREER AT **SPORTING CP**, JOINING **TOTTENHAM HOTSPUR** IN 2014 IN A £4 MILLION TRANSFER?

2   NAME THE BRAZILIAN FORWARD WHO WAS TOP PRIMEIRA LIGA GOALSCORER WITH **BENFICA** BEFORE SPENDING A SEASON ON LOAN AT **SPURS** IN 2020?

3   CAPPED 12 TIMES BY **PORTUGAL**, WHICH MIDFIELDER WON THE PRIMEIRA LIGA AND THE UEFA CHAMPIONS LEAGUE WITH **PORTO** IN 2004 BEFORE JOINING **SPURS**, FOR WHOM HE ONCE FAMOUSLY SCORED A 50-YARD GOAL AGAINST **MANCHESTER UNITED** THAT WAS DISALLOWED? HE LATER WON HONOURS WITH **PORTSMOUTH** AND **RANGERS** BEFORE RETURNING TO PORTUGUESE FOOTBALL.

4   WHICH **SPURS** MANAGER USED TO WORK AS AN INTERPRETER FOR **SIR BOBBY ROBSON** AT **SPORTING CP** AND **PORTO?**

5   NAME THE STRIKER, CAPPED 71 TIMES BY **PORTUGAL**, WHO WON LEAGUE TITLES WITH **PORTO** EITHER SIDE OF A SEASON WITH **TOTTENHAM** IN 2003-04.

6   WHICH **BELGIUM** INTERNATIONAL CENTRAL DEFENDER JOINED **BENFICA** IN 2020 AFTER EIGHT SEASONS AT **SPURS?**

7   NAME THE **SPURS** MANAGER WHO HAD WON FOUR MAJOR TROPHIES IN HIS ONE SEASON AS MANAGER OF **PORTO** IN 2010-11.

GREAVSIE!

JIMMY GREAVES MADE A HABIT OF SCORING ON HIS DEBUT FOR EVERY TEAM ON WHICH HE PLAYED. WHEN HE JOINED **TOTTENHAM HOTSPUR** IN 1961, THE FEE WAS SET AT £99,999, A FIGURE INTENDED TO RELIEVE HIM OF THE PRESSURE OF BECOMING THE FIRST £100,000 FOOTBALLER.
THE ALL-TIME TOP GOALSCORER FOR **SPURS** WITH 266 GOALS IN 379 GAMES, HE SCORED 44 GOALS IN 57 APPEARANCES FOR **ENGLAND** BUT NEVER CAME TO TERMS WITH HIS OMISSION FROM THE SIDE THAT WON THE WORLD CUP ON HOME SOIL IN 1966.

1 HE BEGAN HIS CAREER AT WHICH CLUB, WHERE HE WAS A MEMBER OF **"DRAKE'S DUCKLINGS"** AT THE AGE OF 17?

2 HE MADE HIS **ENGLAND** DEBUT AT THE AGE OF 19 IN 1959 -- WHICH MANAGER GAVE HIM HIS DEBUT FOR **"THE THREE LIONS"?**

3 **GREAVES** SIGNED FOR WHICH ITALIAN SERIE A TEAM IN JUNE OF 1961, LEAVING FOR **SPURS** SIX MONTHS LATER?

4 HOW MANY FA CUPS DID HE WIN IN NINE SEASONS WITH **SPURS?**

5 HE JOINED **WEST HAM UNITED** IN MARCH, 1970, IN A PART-EXCHANGE DEAL THAT TOOK WHICH WORLD CUP WINNER TO **WHITE HART LANE?**

6 IN A FORD ESCORT ALONGSIDE DRIVER **TONY FALL**, HE FINISHED SIXTH OF 96 ENTRANTS IN WHICH 1970 CAR RALLY?

7 HE CAME OUT OF RETIREMENT IN 1977 TO JOIN WHICH ALLIANCE LEAGUE CLUB WHERE HE PLAYED UNDER MANAGER **BARRY FRY?**

8 BETWEEN 1985 AND 1992, HE PRESENTED A SATURDAY LUNCHTIME TV FOOTBALL PROGRAMME IN PARTNERSHIP WITH WHICH FORMER **LIVERPOOL** AND **SCOTLAND** STRIKER?

9 HE APPEARED AS A CAPTAIN, OPPOSITE **ANDY GRAY** AND **EMLYN HUGHES**, ON WHICH TV SPORTS QUIZ SHOW THAT RAN BETWEEN 1980 AND 1990?

A BIT OF A KNEES-UP ...

JOY TURNED TO DESPAIR FOR *GARY MABBUTT* IN THE 1987 FA CUP FINAL. AFTER HE HAD SCORED THE GOAL THAT GAVE *SPURS* A 2-1 LEAD, *COVENTRY CITY* EQUALISED AND FORCED EXTRA-TIME, WHERE A CROSS DEFLECTED OFF *MABBUTT'S* KNEE AND LOOPED OVER *RAY CLEMENCE* IN THE *TOTTENHAM* GOAL TO GIVE *"THE SKY BLUES"* VICTORY. THE OWN GOAL IS STILL SO CELEBRATED BY *COVENTRY* FANS THAT THERE WAS EVEN A *CITY* FANZINE NAMED *"GARY MABBUTT'S KNEE"*.

MABBUTT JOINED *SPURS* FROM *BRISTOL ROVERS* IN 1982. FROM WHICH TEAM HAD THESE OTHER MEMBERS OF *TOTTENHAM'S* 1987 FA CUP FINAL SIDE BEEN RECRUITED?

1 *RAY CLEMENCE*

2 *MITCHELL THOMAS*

3 *STEVE HODGE*

4 *RICHARD GOUGH*

5 *CLIVE ALLEN*

6 *PAUL ALLEN*

7 *CHRIS WADDLE*

8 *OSSIE ARDILES*

9 *NICO CLAESEN*

10 *GARY STEVENS*

CHRIS HUGHTON AND *GLENN HODDLE* HAD GRADUATED FROM *TOTTENHAM'S* YOUTH RANKS.

BORO BOYS

CHRISTIAN ZIEGE ARRIVED AT **TOTTENHAM** IN 2001 WITH A LARGE HAUL OF MEDALS, HAVING WON TWO LEAGUE TITLES AND A UEFA CUP WITH **BAYERN MUNICH**, A SERIE A TITLE WITH **AC MILAN**, A TREBLE OF FA CUP, LEAGUE CUP AND UEFA CUP WITH **LIVERPOOL** AND THE 1996 EUROPEAN CHAMPIONSHIP WITH **GERMANY**. HE SPENT THREE SEASONS AT **WHITE HART LANE** BEFORE A SWANSONG SEASON WITH **BORUSSIA MÖNCHENGLADBACH**, WHERE HE SUBSEQUENTLY JOINED THE COACHING STAFF. HE HAS COACHED **GERMANY** AT U18 AND U19 LEVEL, AS WELL AS MANAGING TEAMS IN GERMANY, SPAIN, THAILAND AND AUSTRIA.

BEFORE JOINING **LIVERPOOL**, **ZIEGE** SPENT A SEASON WITH **MIDDLESBROUGH**. NAME THESE OTHERS WHO HAVE CONNECTIONS TO **SPURS** AND **"THE BORO"**.

1 **EGYPT** STRIKER WHO SPENT THREE SEASONS WITH **MIDDLESBROUGH** AFTER LEAVING **SPURS** IN 2007, HE ALSO PLAYED IN BELGIUM, THE NETHERLANDS, SPAIN, FRANCE AND ITALY.

2 **ENGLAND** MIDFIELDER WHO LAUNCHED HIS CAREER AT **TOTTENHAM**, BECAME **MIDDLESBROUGH'S** MOST-EXPENSIVE SIGNING IN 1995, PLAYED FOR **EVERTON, LIVERPOOL, LEEDS UNITED** AND **NOTTINGHAM FOREST** BEFORE JOINING **HULL CITY**, WHERE HE WAS ALSO BRIEFLY PLAYER/MANAGER.

3 RIGHT-BACK SIGNED TO **SPURS** FROM **SHEFFIELD UNITED** IN 2009, HE WAS LOANED OUT TO **MIDDLESBROUGH, LEICESTER CITY** AND **NORWICH CITY** BEFORE HIS 2015 MOVE TO **SWANSEA CITY**.

4 **TOTTENHAM** RIGHT-BACK WHO WAS LOANED TO **BRENTFORD, MILLWALL** AND **MIDDLESBROUGH** BEFORE JOINING **BRISTOL CITY** IN 2015. HE LASTED JUST 26 DAYS AT HIS NEW CLUB BEFORE HE WAS SOLD TO **FULHAM!** HE JOINED **WEST HAM UNITED** IN 2018.

5 **ENGLAND** CENTRE-BACK WHO WENT FROM **LEEDS UNITED** TO **NEWCASTLE UNITED, REAL MADRID, MIDDLESBROUGH, SPURS** AND **STOKE CITY** BEFORE HE ENDED HIS PLAYING DAYS BACK AT **MIDDLESBROUGH**, WHOM HE SUBSEQUENTLY MANAGED BEFORE TAKING THE **BOURNEMOUTH** JOB IN 2021.

6 ENGLAND LEFT-BACK SIGNED FROM *MIDDLESBROUGH* IN 1964, HE WON MULTIPLE HONOURS WITH *SPURS* INCLUDING THE FA CUP, TWO LEAGUE CUPS AND THE UEFA CUP. BETWEEN 1965 AND 1969 HE MISSED JUST ONE LEAGUE GAME. HE WENT ON TO MANAGE *DARLINGTON, TORQUAY UNITED* AND *HARTLEPOOL UNITED* BEFORE HIS 1991 DEATH AT THE AGE OF 47.

7 FORMER *ASTON VILLA* AND *MIDDLESBROUGH* CENTRE-BACK WHO WAS THE *TOTTENHAM U23* MANAGER WHEN HE SUFFERED A FATAL HEART ATTACK ON THE TRAINING GROUND IN 2017.

8 *TOTTENHAM* MIDFIELDER WHO WENT ON TO MANAGE *SPURS, MIDDLESBROUGH, BARCELONA, ENGLAND* AND MORE.

9 ENGLAND STAR WHOSE CLUBS INCLUDED *NEWCASTLE UNITED, SPURS, LAZIO, RANGERS, MIDDLESBROUGH* AND MORE.

10 DEFENDER CAPPED SEVEN TIMES BY *ENGLAND*, HE LEFT *SPURS* FOR *CHARLTON ATHLETIC* IN 2001 AND LATER PLAYED FOR *MIDDLESBROUGH, ASTON VILLA* AND *QPR*.

MAYBE IT'S BECAUSE I'M A LONDONER

TERRY VENABLES -- WHO PLAYED FOR AND LATER MANAGED **SPURS** -- SET THE RECORD OF BEING THE FIRST MAN CAPPED AT EVERY INTERNATIONAL LEVEL FOR **ENGLAND** -- SCHOOLBOY, YOUTH, AMATEUR, UNDER-23 AND SENIOR. HIS TWO FULL **ENGLAND** CAPS WERE GAINED IN 1964. AT CLUB LEVEL, HE WON A LEAGUE CUP WITH **CHELSEA**, THE FA CUP WITH **TOTTENHAM** AND GAINED PROMOTION TO THE TOP FLIGHT WITH **QUEENS PARK RANGERS**, BEFORE ENDING HIS PLAYING DAYS AT **CRYSTAL PALACE**, WHERE **MALCOLM ALLISON** GAVE HIM THE COACHING JOB THAT LAUNCHED **TERRY'S** MANAGEMENT CAREER.

IDENTIFY THESE **SPURS** MANAGERS BY THE CLUBS THEY PLAYED FOR:

1   ASTON VILLA, CHELSEA, ARSENAL, MANCHESTER UNITED, PORTSMOUTH, CRYSTAL PALACE, CALIFORNIA SURF

2   WEST HAM UNITED, AFC BOURNEMOUTH, BRENTFORD, SEATTLE SOUNDERS, AP LEAMINGTON, PHOENIX FIRE

3   WATFORD, NORWICH CITY, BLACKBURN ROVERS, TOTTENHAM HOTSPUR, PORTSMOUTH, COVENTRY CITY

4   RIO AVE, BELENENSES, SESIMBRA, COMÉRCIO E INDÚSTRIA

5   SPURS, MONACO, SWINDON TOWN, CHELSEA

6   SAINT-ÉTIENNE, MONTPELLIER, LISIEUX

7   NEWELL'S OLD BOYS, ESPANYOL, PARIS SAINT-GERMAIN, BORDEAUX

8   GRASSHOPPER, LAUSANNE-SPORT, NEUCHÂTEL XAMAX, VFL BOCHUM, ST. GALLEN, LUGANO, YVERDON-SPORT

9   ADO DEN HAAG, BAYERN MUNICH, TWENTE, WEST BROMWICH ALBION, COVENTRY CITY

10 LIVERPOOL, NORWICH CITY, BOURNEMOUTH,
CARDIFF CITY, CHESTER

11 INSTITUTO DE CÓRDOBA, BELGRANO, HURACÁN, SPURS,
PARIS SAINT-GERMAIN, ST GEORGE FC, BLACKBURN
ROVERS, QUEENS PARK RANGERS, FORT LAUDERDALE
STRIKERS, SWINDON TOWN

12 VITÓRIA GUIMARÃES, VILA REAL, DEPORTIVO LA CORUÑA,
MÉRIDA, OSASUNA, PORTO, DYNAMO MOSCOW, AVES

13 NOTTINGHAM FOREST,
LUTON TOWN,
SHREWSBURY TOWN,
EXETER CITY,
PETERBOROUGH
UNITED

FA CUP KINGS

THE FIRST PLAYER TO APPEAR IN FIVE **FA CUP** FINALS, INCLUDING FOUR AS AN **ARSENAL** PLAYER -- WITH WHOM HE ALSO GAINED THREE **LEAGUE CHAMPIONSHIP** MEDALS -- **ENGLAND** WINGER **JOE HULME** WAS ALSO A TOP-CLASS BATSMAN WITH **MIDDLESEX** AND EXCELLED AT BOTH BILLIARDS AND GOLF. HE WORKED AS A POLICEMAN DURING THE SECOND WORLD WAR, AFTER WHICH HE MANAGED **TOTTENHAM** FOR FOUR YEARS BEFORE BECOMING A RESPECTED SPORTS WRITER.

1 NAME THE FOUR MEMBERS OF THE **SPURS** TEAMS THAT WON THE FA CUP IN 1981 AND 1982 WHO LATER MANAGED **TOTTENHAM**.

2 WHICH **TOTTENHAM** MANAGER WON THE FA CUP AS A PLAYER WITH **ARSENAL** IN 1971?

3 NAME THE **SPURS** MANAGER WHO HAD PLAYED ON THE **TOTTENHAM** TEAM THAT WON THE FA CUP IN 1967.

4 WHICH CENTRAL DEFENDER WON FOUR FA CUPS WITH TWO TEAMS AFTER LEAVING **SPURS** ON A FREE TRANSFER IN 2001?

5 WHICH TWO **SPURS** PLAYERS WON THE FA CUP IN 1967 PLAYING AGAINST THEIR FORMER TEAM?

6 WHICH FA CUP-WINNING **TOTTENHAM** MANAGER ALSO MANAGED A TEAM THAT LOST TO **TOTTENHAM** IN AN FA CUP FINAL?

7 WHICH SUBSEQUENT **TOTTENHAM** PLAYER SCORED AGAINST **SPURS** IN THE 1982 FA CUP FINAL?

8 WHICH PLAYER WON FA CUPS WITH **SPURS** AND **LIVERPOOL?**

9 NAME THE FOUR **TOTTENHAM** MANAGERS WHO WON THE FA CUP AS MANAGER OF ANOTHER TEAM.

10 WHAT FA CUP FINAL RECORD IS SHARED BETWEEN **JOHN CAMERON** WITH **TOTTENHAM HOTSPUR** IN 1901 AND **KENNY DALGLISH** WITH **LIVERPOOL** IN 1986?

LE GARDIEN

SON OF A LAWYER MOTHER AND A MONTE CARLO-BASED BANKER FATHER, *HUGO LLORIS* WAS BORN INTO PRIVILEGE. AS A YOUNGSTER, HE EXCELLED AT TENNIS BUT OPTED TO PURSUE FOOTBALL, HAVING JOINED THE YOUTH ACADEMY AT *NICE* AT THE AGE OF 10. HE REPRESENTED *FRANCE* AT VARIOUS YOUTH LEVELS, MADE HIS SENIOR DEBUT IN 2008, WON THE FIFA WORLD CUP TEN YEARS LATER AND IS NOW THE MOST-CAPPED GOALKEEPER IN THE HISTORY OF THE *FRANCE* TEAM.

NAME THESE *FRANCE* INTERNATIONALS WHO HAVE PLAYED FOR *SPURS*:

1 MIDFIELDER WHO JOINED *SPURS* IN 2016 AFTER HE WAS RELEGATED WITH *NEWCASTLE UNITED*. HE JOINED *WATFORD* IN 2021.

2 CAPPED SEVEN TIMES, A DEFENSIVE MIDFIELDER WHO BEGAN HIS CAREER AT *TOULOUSE*, THEN SPENT TWO SEASONS WITH *TOTTENHAM HOTSPUR* BEFORE JOINING *WATFORD* IN 2015. AFTER SIGNING FOR *VILLARREAL* IN LATE 2020, HE WAS NAMED MAN OF THE MATCH IN THE 2021 EUROPA LEAGUE FINAL VICTORY OVER *MANCHESTER UNITED*.

3 A FIRST DIVISION AND UEFA INTERTOTO CUP WINNER WITH *FULHAM*, A STRIKER WHO WON MULTIPLE HONOURS IN HIS FIVE SEASONS WITH *MANCHESTER UNITED*, WHO THEN SPENT THREE SEASONS WITH *EVERTON*. SIX MONTHS WITH *TOTTENHAM* IN 2012 WAS FOLLOWED BY BRIEF SPELLS WITH *SUNDERLAND* AND *LAZIO*.

4 A LEAGUE AND CUP WINNER WITH *PARIS SAINT-GERMAIN*, HE JOINED *TOTTENHAM* FROM *NEWCASTLE UNITED* IN 1997. HE WENT ON TO WIN THE LEAGUE CUP IN 1998-99, THE SAME SEASON HE WAS VOTED PFA PLAYERS' PLAYER OF THE YEAR AND FWA FOOTBALLER OF THE YEAR.

5 CENTRE-BACK CAPPED 84 TIMES, HE WON TWO LEAGUE TITLES AND THE LEAGUE CUP WITH *CHELSEA*, WON AND LOST THE *ARSENAL* CAPTAINCY AND THEN JOINED *TOTTENHAM* IN 2010.

6 MIDFIELDER SIGNED TO *SPURS* FROM *LYON* IN 2019 IN A DEAL WORTH £55.5 MILLION PLUS UP TO £9 MILLION IN ADD-ONS.

7 CENTRE-BACK WHO WON THE 2008 LEAGUE CUP IN HIS FIRST SPELL AT **SPURS**, SPENT TWO YEARS WITH **PORTSMOUTH**, RETURNED TO **TOTTENHAM** BEFORE, AFTER SIX INJURY-PLAGUED SEASONS, MOVING ON TO **SUNDERLAND** AND **WATFORD**.

BRAVEHEARTS!

BORN IN SWEDEN, RAISED IN SOUTH AFRICA, **RICHARD GOUGH** WON A
LEAGUE TITLE AND REACHED THE SEMI-FINALS OF THE EUROPEAN CUP
WITH **DUNDEE UNITED** BEFORE JOINING **TOTTENHAM** IN 1986. AFTER
CAPTAINING THE TEAM IN THE 1987 FA CUP FINAL, HE RETURNED TO
SCOTLAND TO SIGN FOR **RANGERS**. SFWA FOOTBALLER OF THE YEAR IN
1988-89, HE CAPTAINED **RANGERS** TO NINE CONSECUTIVE LEAGUE TITLES.
HE WON 61 CAPS FOR **SCOTLAND**, AND PLAYED IN TWO WORLD CUPS.

IDENTIFY THESE OTHER **SPURS** PLAYERS WHO REPRESENTED **SCOTLAND:**

1 22 CAPS 1957-1965: MIDFIELDER WHO WON LEAGUE TITLES AS A
PLAYER WITH **HEART OF MIDLOTHIAN, SPURS** AND **DERBY
COUNTY**, AND AS A MANAGER WITH **DERBY COUNTY**, EGYPT'S
ZAMALEK SC AND KUWAIT'S **AL-ARABI SC**.

2 22 CAPS 1959-1964: INSIDE-FORWARD WHO LOST HIS LIFE IN 1964 AT
THE AGE OF 27.

3 22 CAPS 1963-1971: STRIKER WHO WON A LEAGUE TITLE WITH
DUNDEE, BEFORE WINNING THE FA CUP, TWO LEAGUE CUPS AND THE
UEFA CUP IN HIS TEN YEARS WITH **TOTTENHAM**.

4 50 CAPS 2007-2016: SIGNED FROM **RANGERS** IN 2008, A RIGHT-
BACK WHO WON THE 2008 LEAGUE CUP WITH **SPURS** BEFORE
SPENDING EIGHT SEASONS WITH **ASTON VILLA**.

5 36 CAPS 1995-1999: CENTRAL DEFENDER WHO ROSE FROM THE
FOURTH DIVISION TO THE PREMIERSHIP WITH **SWINDON TOWN**
BEFORE SPENDING SIX YEARS AT **WHITE HART LANE**, HE LATER
PLAYED FOR **ASTON VILLA** AND **NOTTINGHAM FOREST** BEFORE
EMBARKING ON A CAREER IN MANAGEMENT.

6 43 CAPS 1987-1998: STRIKER SIGNED FROM **CHELSEA** IN 1993, HE
SCORED **TOTTENHAM'S** FIRST PREMIER LEAGUE GOAL.

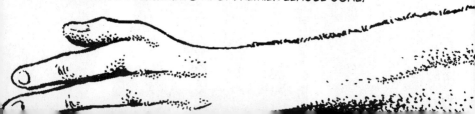

7   27 CAPS 1980-1986: LEAGUE TITLE WINNER WITH *ABERDEEN*, STRIKER WHO WON TWO FA CUPS AND THE UEFA CUP WITH *SPURS* AND LA LIGA WITH *BARCELONA*.

8   13 CAPS 1980-1983: HAVING WON THE FA CUP AND UEFA CUP WITH *IPSWICH TOWN*, HE WON THE 1984 UEFA CUP WITH *TOTTENHAM* BEFORE JOINING *MANCHESTER UNITED*.

9   28 CAPS 1997-2003: GOALKEEPER WHOSE CAREER INCLUDED SPELLS WITH *WIMBLEDON*, *SPURS*, *CHELSEA* AND *LEEDS UNITED* AND SEVEN YEARS WITH *DONCASTER ROVERS*.

10   28 CAPS 1958-1965: *TOTTENHAM'S* NO. 1 GOALKEEPER IN THE 1961 DOUBLE-WINNING TEAM.

CRAZY DAYS!

HAVING LAUNCHED HIS CAREER AT **SPURS**, **TERRY GIBSON** PLAYED FOR **COVENTRY CITY** AND **MANCHESTER UNITED** BEFORE LANDING AT **WIMBLEDON** IN 1987, WHERE HE PLAYED IN THE TRUCULENT "*CRAZY GANG*" THAT WON THE FA CUP IN 1988. HE SPENT SIX YEARS AT THE CLUB, WHICH WAS DISSOLVED IN 2004 AND REFORMED IN MILTON KEYNES AS **MK DONS**. **GIBSON** WAS LATER ASSISTANT TO HIS FORMER **WIMBLEDON** TEAMMATE **LAWRIE SANCHEZ** WITH **NORTHERN IRELAND**.

1 WHICH MIDFIELDER WAS SIGNED FROM **MK DONS** FOR AN INITIAL FEE OF £5 MILLION IN EARLY 2015 AND IMMEDIATELY LOANED BACK TO **THE DONS** FOR THE REMAINDER OF THE SEASON?

2 WHICH **SPURS** GREAT WENT ON TO MANAGE **WIMBLEDON, NOTTINGHAM FOREST, LUTON, NEWCASTLE** AND MORE?

3 HAVING SPENT MUCH OF HIS SEVEN YEARS WITH **TOTTENHAM** OUT ON LOAN -- INCLUDING A SPELL WITH **MK DONS** -- NAME THE ACADEMY GRADUATE RIGHT-BACK WHO JOINED **BOURNEMOUTH** IN 2014 AND BECAME AN ESTABLISHED FIRST TEAM REGULAR.

4 WHICH WINGER, HAVING LAUNCHED HIS CAREER AT **SPURS**, WAS GIVEN HIS **ENGLAND** DEBUT IN 2013 BY ROY HODGSON, WHO LATER MANAGED HIM FOR FOUR SEASONS AT **CRYSTAL PALACE?**

5 WHO WAS **WIMBLEDON'S** FIRST MILLION POUND SIGNING, AN UNCOMPROMISING HARDMAN WHO COST **SPURS** £5 MILLION IN 2000 AND WENT ON TO PLAY FOR **LEICESTER, MANCHESTER CITY, CHARLTON ATHLETIC** AND **IPSWICH TOWN?**

6 NAME THE **SPURS** YOUTH TEAM GRADUATE, A CENTRAL MIDFIELDER, WHO SPENT THE EARLY YEARS OF HIS CAREER ON LOAN AT VARIOUS CLUBS -- INCLUDING **MK DONS** AND **LEEDS UNITED** -- WON HIS FIRST **ENGLAND** CAP IN 2012, ESTABLISHED HIS REPUTATION AT **HULL CITY** AND WAS A £10 MILLION **WEST BROM** SIGNING IN 2017.

7 WHICH FORMER **WIMBLEDON** INSIDE-FORWARD HAD TWO SPELLS AS **SPURS** MANAGER, IN 1984-86 AND IN THE 1991-92 SEASON?

8 WHICH **WIMBLEDON** DEFENDER WAS **TOTTENHAM'S** RECORD SIGNING WHEN HE JOINED IN A £4 MILLION TRANSFER IN 1999?

9 NAME THE GOALKEEPER WHO SPENT THE FIRST DOZEN YEARS OF HIS CAREER AT **WIMBLEDON** BEFORE SUPPLANTING **IAN WALKER** AS FIRST CHOICE WITH **SPURS** AFTER SIGNING IN 2000.

10 AN FA CUP WINNER WITH **WIMBLEDON** IN 1988, WHICH **ENGLAND** INTERNATIONAL WON THE LEAGUE CUP WITH **LIVERPOOL** IN 1995, SPENT FOUR INJURY-RAVAGED YEARS AT **SPURS** AND ENDED HIS PLAYING DAYS WITH A SPELL AT **IPSWICH TOWN?**

"ARCHIGOLES"

18-YEAR-OLD **STEVE ARCHIBALD** WAS WORKING AS AN APPRENTICE MECHANIC WHEN HE WAS SPOTTED AND RECRUITED BY **CLYDE** MANAGER **STAN ANDERSON**. HE WAS STILL PLAYING PART-TIME WHEN **SCOTLAND** AND **CELTIC** GREAT **BILLY MCNEILL** TOOK OVER THE REINS ... AND WHEN **MCNEILL** WAS APPOINTED MANAGER OF **ABERDEEN** A FEW MONTHS LATER, HE TOOK THE GLASGOW-BORN YOUNGSTER WITH HIM, LAUNCHING THE TEENAGER INTO THE BIG TIME.

1 WHO SUCCEEDED **MCNEILL** AS **ABERDEEN** MANAGER IN 1978?

2 AFTER WINNING THE SCOTTISH LEAGUE TITLE WITH **ABERDEEN** IN 1980, **ARCHIBALD** JOINED **SPURS** FOR £800,000. WHO WAS THE **TOTTENHAM** MANAGER WHO SIGNED HIM?

3 **ARCHIBALD**, WHO WON TWO FA CUPS WITH **SPURS**, SCORED IN THE 1982 LEAGUE CUP FINAL DEFEAT AT THE HANDS OF WHICH TEAM?

4 HE WAS CAPPED 27 TIMES BY **SCOTLAND** BETWEEN 1980 AND 1986, AND PLAYED IN TWO WORLD CUPS. CAN YOU NAME THE TWO **SCOTLAND** MANAGERS UNDER WHOM HE PLAYED?

5 IN WHAT WOULD PROVE TO BE HIS FINAL GAME FOR THE CLUB, **ARCHIBALD** SCORED IN THE PENALTY SHOOT-OUT THAT GAVE **SPURS** VICTORY OVER WHICH TEAM IN THE 1984 UEFA CUP FINAL?

6 WHO WAS THE MANAGER WHO SIGNED **STEVE ARCHIBALD** TO **BARCELONA** IN 1984 IN A £1,150,000 DEAL?

7 **"ARCHIGOLES"** HELPED **BARCELONA** TO A FIRST LEAGUE TITLE IN 11 YEARS IN HIS DEBUT SEASON, AND THEN THE 1986 EUROPEAN CUP FINAL, WHERE THEY LOST ON PENALTY KICKS TO WHICH TEAM?

8 HE SPENT MUCH OF HIS FINAL **BARCELONA** SEASON OUT ON LOAN, PLAYING UNDER **DON MACKAY** AT WHICH ENGLISH CLUB?

9 NAME ONE OF THE FIVE SCOTTISH CLUBS HE PLAYED FOR AFTER LEAVING **BARCELONA** IN 1988, ONE OF WHICH SAW HIM APPOINTED PLAYER/MANAGER.

10   IN 1992, HE PLAYED BRIEFLY UNDER **DON MACKAY** ONCE MORE AT WHICH LONDON CLUB?

11   IN 1996, HE TURNED OUT FOR A TEAM CALLED **HOME FARM EVERTON** -- IN WHICH CITY WAS THAT CLUB BASED?

THE PERFECT ONE

DURING HIS FIRST SPELL AS *CHELSEA* MANAGER, *JOSÉ MOURINHO* PROCLAIMED HIMSELF A *"SPECIAL ONE"*, A SOUBRIQUET THAT WAS GLEEFULLY ADOPTED BY THE MEDIA. WHEN *JUANDE RAMOS* TOOK OVER AS *SPURS* MANAGER IN OCTOBER OF 2007, HAVING ENJOYED HUGE TRIUMPHS WITH *SEVILLA*, HIS DETERMINATION TO SHAKE UP EVERY ASPECT OF THE CLUB SAW THE PRESS LABEL HIM *"THE RUTHLESS ONE"*. HIS EARLY SUCCESSES WITH *SPURS* EARNED HIM THE NICKNAME *"THE PERFECT ONE"* WITHIN THE CLUB ... BUT THINGS WENT RAPIDLY DOWNHILL IN HIS SECOND SEASON AND HE WAS AXED, HIS *TOTTENHAM* TENURE HAVING LASTED TWO DAYS SHY OF A YEAR.

1 HAVING SPENT 15 YEARS PAYING HIS DUES AT A STRING OF PROGRESSIVELY LARGER SPANISH CLUBS, *RAMOS* WAS APPOINTED BOSS OF *SEVILLA* IN 2005. HE WON THE UEFA CUP IN HIS FIRST SEASON, DEFEATING WHICH ENGLISH SIDE 4-0 IN THE FINAL?

2 *SEVILLA* WON THE 2006 UEFA SUPER CUP, BEATING CHAMPIONS LEAGUE WINNERS *BARCELONA*, MANAGED BY WHICH DUTCHMAN?

3 *SEVILLA* RETAINED THE UEFA CUP IN 2007, BEATING WHICH SPANISH SIDE, MANAGED BY *ERNESTO VALVERDE*, IN THE FINAL?

4 BEFORE *JUANDE RAMOS* WAS INSTALLED AS *TOTTENHAM* MANAGER IN 2007, *SPURS* STALWART *CLIVE ALLEN* BRIEFLY HELD DOWN THE FORT AS CARETAKER BOSS FOLLOWING THE DISMISSAL OF WHICH DUTCH MANAGER?

5 WHO WAS ASSISTANT MANAGER TO *RAMOS* AT *SPURS?*

6 WHO DID *TOTTENHAM* CRUSH 6-2 ON AGGREGATE IN THE 2008 LEAGUE CUP SEMI-FINAL?

7 *RAMOS* GUIDED *SPURS* TO A 2-1 VICTORY OVER *CHELSEA* IN THE 2008 LEAGUE CUP FINAL -- WHO SCORED THE WINNING GOAL?

8 *RAMOS* WAS DISMISSED IN OCTOBER, 2008 -- WHO SUCCEEDED HIM AS *TOTTENHAM* MANAGER?

9 LATER THAT YEAR, *RAMOS* REPLACED *BERND SCHUSTER* AS MANAGER OF WHICH TEAM?

10 AMONG THE PLAYERS SIGNED TO *SPURS* DURING THE 12 MONTHS *RAMOS* WAS IN CHARGE WAS *DAVID BENTLEY*, A £15 MILLION ACQUISITION WITH THE POTENTIAL OF A FURTHER £2 MILLION IN ADD-ONS, SIGNED FROM WHICH CLUB?

THE BOYS OF '67

BRIAN CLOUGH ONCE DECLARED THAT **DAVE MACKAY** WAS **TOTTENHAM'S** GREATEST-EVER PLAYER. HIS ADMIRATION FOR THE SCOTTISH INTERNATIONAL WAS CONFIRMED WHEN HE SIGNED THE 33-YEAR-OLD MIDFIELD GENERAL TO **DERBY COUNTY** IN 1968, A YEAR AFTER **MACKAY** HAD CAPTAINED THE **SPURS** SIDE THAT WON THE FA CUP.

WHICH CLUB DID THE FOLLOWING MEMBERS OF THE 1967 FA CUP-WINNING TEAM JOIN AFTER LEAVING **TOTTENHAM HOTSPUR?**

1   *PAT JENNINGS*

2   *JOE KINNEAR*

3   *ALAN MULLERY*

4   *MIKE ENGLAND*

5   *JIMMY ROBERTSON*

6   *JIMMY GREAVES*

7   *ALAN GILZEAN*

8   *TERRY VENABLES*

9   *FRANK SAUL*

10   *CLIFF JONES*

TEAM MEMBER **CYRIL KNOWLES** RETIRED WHEN HIS **TOTTENHAM** PLAYING DAYS ENDED.

THEM'S THE BREAKS!

FOLLOWING HIS ARRIVAL AT **WHITE HART LANE** IN FEBRUARY, 1958, **CLIFF JONES** STRUGGLED TO RECAPTURE THE FORM THAT HAD CONVINCED **SPURS** TO PAY A RECORD £35,000 TO SIGN HIM FROM **SWANSEA TOWN**. A BROKEN LEG IN THE SUMMER FURTHER HAMPERED HIS PROGRESS ... BUT AFTER RETURNING TO ACTION IN DECEMBER OF THAT YEAR, THE **WALES** WINGER FOUND HIS FORM. HE SCORED 25 GOALS THE FOLLOWING SEASON AND WAS A VITAL MEMBER OF THE TEAM THAT CAPTURED THE DOUBLE IN 1960-61. IN HIS DECADE WITH **TOTTENHAM**, **JONES** SCORED 159 GOALS IN 378 GAMES.

1 NAME THE MIDFIELDER WHO BROKE HIS LEFT LEG TWICE IN NINE MONTHS BUT RETURNED TO WIN A THIRD FA CUP MEDAL AND BE NAMED 1969 FWA FOOTBALLER OF THE YEAR.

2 NAME THE GOALKEEPER WHO DISLOCATED HIS LEFT ELBOW IN A 3-0 LOSS AWAY TO **BRIGHTON & HOVE ALBION** IN 2019.

3 WHICH WELSH WINGER SUFFERED A BROKEN LEG ON A SUMMER 1963 TOUR OF SOUTH AFRICA THAT FORCED HIS EARLY RETIREMENT?

4 IN 2012, WHILE ON LOAN AT WHICH CLUB MANAGED BY **CHRIS HUGHTON**, DID **HARRY KANE** FRACTURE A METATARSAL?

5 WHO BROKE HIS FOREARM IN A 2020 GAME AGAINST **ASTON VILLA** YET STAYED ON THE FIELD AND SCORED A BRACE, EVEN THOUGH THE INJURY WOULD LATER REQUIRE SURGERY AND A LENGTHY LAY-OFF?

6 NAME THE **SPURS** BOSS WHOSE PLAYING CAREER WAS ENDED BY A FRACTURED SKULL THAT RESULTED IN 45 STAPLES, A SIX-INCH SCAR AND 14 METAL PLATES IN HIS SKULL HELD IN PLACE BY 28 SCREWS.

7 WHICH HARDMAN DEFENDER BROKE HIS LEG ON HIS **SPURS** DEBUT IN 1986 PLAYING AGAINST **LIVERPOOL** -- A CLUB HE WOULD JOIN IN THE 1990S FOLLOWING HIS SECOND SPELL WITH **TOTTENHAM**?

8 WHOSE BROKEN LEG AGAINST **BIRMINGHAM** IN 2009 RULED HIM OUT OF **CROATIA'S** WORLD CUP QUALIFIER AGAINST **ENGLAND**?

9 DESPITE AN 18-MONTH BATTLE TO RECOVER, WHICH *ENGLAND* INTERNATIONAL, A WINNER OF MULTIPLE HONOURS DURING HIS 11 YEARS AT *TOTTENHAM*, WAS FORCED TO RETIRE FOLLOWING FRACTURES OF TIBIA AND FIBULA IN A FRIENDLY GAME AGAINST A *HUNGARIAN SELECT XI* AT *WHITE HART LANE* IN 1965?

MAGIC CHRIS

WHILE WORKING IN A SAUSAGE SEASONING FACTORY, **CHRIS WADDLE** HAD UNSUCCESSFUL TRIALS WITH **SUNDERLAND** AND **COVENTRY CITY**, BEFORE HE WAS FINALLY TAKEN ON BY **NEWCASTLE UNITED** AT THE AGE OF 19. CAPPED 62 TIMES BY **ENGLAND**, HE WAS STILL PLAYING SEMI-PRO FOOTBALL IN HIS MID-FIFTIES!

1 NAME THE TWO MANAGERS HE PLAYED UNDER AT **NEWCASTLE UNITED** BETWEEN 1980 AND 1985.

2 **WADDLE** WAS 24 YEARS OLD WHEN HE EARNED HIS FIRST **ENGLAND** U-21 CAP IN 1985, A FEW WEEKS BEFORE WHICH MANAGER GAVE HIM A FULL **ENGLAND** DEBUT?

3 HE JOINED **TOTTENHAM** IN THE SUMMER OF 1985 -- NAME THE THREE MANAGERS UNDER WHOM HE PLAYED BEFORE HIS DEPARTURE FOR FRANCE FOUR YEARS LATER.

4 HE JOINED **OLYMPIQUE DE MARSEILLE** IN 1989 AND WON THREE CONSECUTIVE LEAGUE TITLES. HE ALSO PLAYED IN THE 1991 EUROPEAN CUP FINAL WHERE **MARSEILLE** LOST TO WHICH TEAM?

5 WHICH **ENGLAND** INTERNATIONAL PLAYED ALONGSIDE **WADDLE** AT **MARSEILLE** FOR A SEASON BEFORE RETURNING TO **RANGERS?**

6 WHO WAS THE MANAGER WHO SIGNED **WADDLE** TO **SHEFFIELD WEDNESDAY** IN A £1 MILLION TRANSFER IN 1992?

7 **SHEFFIELD WEDNESDAY** REACHED THE FINALS OF BOTH THE FA CUP AND THE LEAGUE CUP IN **WADDLE'S** DEBUT SEASON, LOSING TO THE SAME TEAM IN BOTH GAMES. WHO WERE THE OPPONENTS?

8 NAME ONE OF THE THREE TEAMS HE PLAYED FOR -- ONE IN SCOTLAND AND TWO IN ENGLAND -- IN THE 1996-97 SEASON.

9 HE WAS APPOINTED PLAYER/MANAGER OF WHICH CLUB IN 1997?

THE BOYS IN GREEN

THE MOST-CAPPED PLAYER IN THE HISTORY OF THE **REPUBLIC OF IRELAND** -- **ROBBIE KEANE** WAS CAPPED 146 TIMES BETWEEN 1998 AND 2016 -- AND WITH 68 GOALS, HE IS ALSO HIS COUNTRY'S LEADING GOALSCORER.

IDENTIFY THESE OTHER **SPURS** PLAYERS WHO WORE THE GREEN SHIRT:

1   CAPPED 44 TIMES, A LEAGUE CUP WINNER WITH **SPURS** IN 1999, A RIGHT-BACK WHO WENT ON TO PLAY FOR **NEWCASTLE UNITED** AND CAPTAIN **BIRMINGHAM CITY.**

2   CAPPED 29 TIMES, A MIDFIELDER WHO BEGAN HIS CAREER WITH FIVE SEASONS AT **NOTTINGHAM FOREST** FROM 2000 AND ENDED HIS PLAYING CAREER IN 2016 AFTER RETURNING FOR FIVE MORE SEASONS. IN BETWEEN, HE PLAYED FOR **SPURS, CHARLTON ATHLETIC, SUNDERLAND, SHEFFIELD UNITED** AND **BLACKPOOL.**

3   CAPPED 39 TIMES, RIGHT-BACK WHO BEGAN HIS PROFESSIONAL CAREER AT **SPURS** AND ALSO PLAYED FOR **SOUTHEND UNITED, QUEENS PARK RANGERS, WATFORD, BIRMINGHAM CITY, STOKE CITY, FULHAM** AND **READING** BEFORE JOINING HIS FINAL CLUB, **ROTHERHAM UNITED** IN 2015.

4   HAVING WON TWO FA CUPS AND THE UEFA CUP IN THE EARLY 1980S WITH **SPURS** AND WON 53 CAPS, HE EMBARKED ON A COACHING CAREER THAT SAW HIM APPOINTED CARETAKER AT **TOTTENHAM** AND MANAGER OF TEAMS INCLUDING **NEWCASTLE UNITED, NORWICH CITY, BRIGHTON & HOVE ALBION** AND MORE.

5   CAPPED 34 TIMES, HE SPENT THE EARLY PART OF HIS CAREER WITH **LUTON TOWN** AND **SPURS** BEFORE JOINING **NORWICH CITY** IN 2004. IN SIX SEASONS WITH **"THE CANARIES"**, THE **"GINGER PELÉ"** WAS VOTED PLAYER OF THE YEAR AND WON THE LEAGUE ONE TITLE IN 2010. HE SUBSEQUENTLY PLAYED FOR **CHARLTON ATHLETIC** AND **WYCOMBE WANDERERS.**

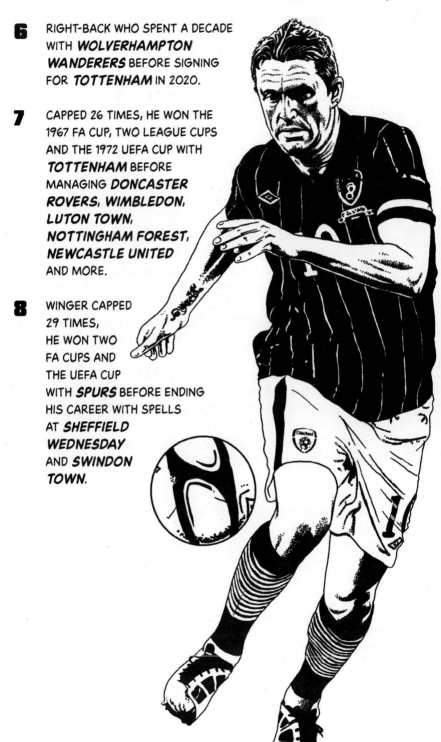

6 RIGHT-BACK WHO SPENT A DECADE WITH **WOLVERHAMPTON WANDERERS** BEFORE SIGNING FOR **TOTTENHAM** IN 2020.

7 CAPPED 26 TIMES, HE WON THE 1967 FA CUP, TWO LEAGUE CUPS AND THE 1972 UEFA CUP WITH **TOTTENHAM** BEFORE MANAGING **DONCASTER ROVERS, WIMBLEDON, LUTON TOWN, NOTTINGHAM FOREST, NEWCASTLE UNITED** AND MORE.

8 WINGER CAPPED 29 TIMES, HE WON TWO FA CUPS AND THE UEFA CUP WITH **SPURS** BEFORE ENDING HIS CAREER WITH SPELLS AT **SHEFFIELD WEDNESDAY** AND **SWINDON TOWN.**

HARRY'S GAME

AS A VERY YOUNG BOY, *HARRY KANE* PLAYED FOR *RIDGEWAY ROVERS* AND WAS ON THE BOOKS AT *ARSENAL* AS AN EIGHT-YEAR-OLD. HE WAS SUBSEQUENTLY REJECTED BY *SPURS* AND HAD A SPELL WITH *WATFORD* BEFORE *TOTTENHAM* RECONSIDERED AND HE JOINED THE *TOTTENHAM* YOUTH ACADEMY AT THE AGE OF 11.

1 NAME ONE OF THE FOUR CLUBS WHERE *KANE* PLAYED ON LOAN DURING THE EARLY DAYS OF HIS PROFESSIONAL CAREER.

2 HE SCORED HIS FIRST PROFESSIONAL HAT-TRICK IN 2014 WHEN *SPURS* BEAT WHICH GREEK TEAM 5-1 IN THE UEFA EUROPA LEAGUE? *(THE GAME WAS ALSO NOTEWORTHY BECAUSE KANE PLAYED IN GOAL FOR THE LAST FEW MINUTES AFTER LLORIS WAS SENT OFF!)*

3 *KANE* SCORED HIS FIRST PREMIER LEAGUE HAT-TRICK IN A 4-3 HOME WIN OVER WHICH FORMER LOAN CLUB IN MARCH, 2015?

4 HE SCORED 80 SECONDS INTO HIS *ENGLAND* DEBUT AFTER COMING ON AS A SUBSTITUTE FOR *WAYNE ROONEY* IN A 4-0 UEFA EURO 2016 QUALIFIER WIN AGAINST WHICH COUNTRY?

5 HE SCORED HIS FIRST *ENGLAND* HAT-TRICK WHEN HE CAPTAINED THE TEAM THAT BEAT WHICH COUNTRY 6-1 AT THE 2018 WORLD CUP?

6 AT THE 2018 TOURNAMENT, HE BECAME THE FIRST *ENGLAND* PLAYER TO WIN THE FIFA GOLDEN BOOT SINCE WHICH TOTTENHAM FORWARD IN 1986?

7 HE SCORED TWO MORE HAT-TRICKS FOR *ENGLAND* IN EURO 2020 QUALIFYING GAMES -- NAME ONE OF THOSE TWO OPPONENTS.

8 IN 2015, HIS *TOTTENHAM* SQUAD NUMBER WAS CHANGED FROM *18* TO THE MORE ICONIC NUMBER *10* PREVIOUSLY WORN BY WHICH DEPARTING AFRICAN STRIKER?

9 HIS 25 GOALS IN 2015-16 MADE HIM *TOTTENHAM'S* FIRST PREMIER LEAGUE GOLDEN BOOT WINNER SINCE WHICH PLAYER IN 1993?

10 IN 2021, ON THE WAY TO WINNING HIS THIRD PREMIER LEAGUE GOLDEN BOOT, HE OVERTOOK WHICH PLAYER TO BECOME THE SECOND-HIGHEST GOALSCORER IN ***TOTTENHAM'S*** HISTORY?

11 HIS GOAL AGAINST ***ANDORRA*** IN LATE 2021 WAS HIS 40TH GOAL FOR ***ENGLAND***, EQUALLING THE TALLY OF WHICH FORMER ***LIVERPOOL*** AND ***REAL MADRID*** STRIKER -- A BENCHMARK ***KANE*** SURPASSED THREE DAYS LATER WITH A GOAL AGAINST ***POLAND?***

SUPER PAV

ON THE BACK OF HIS FORM IN THE *GUUS HIDDINK RUSSIA* TEAM THAT REACHED THE SEMI-FINALS OF EURO 2008, *ROMAN PAVLYUCHENKO* JOINED *TOTTENHAM* FROM *SPARTAK MOSCOW* IN A £13.7 MILLION DEAL. WITHIN WEEKS OF THE RUSSIAN STRIKER'S ARRIVAL AT THE LANE, *JUANDE RAMOS* WAS REPLACED AS MANAGER BY *HARRY REDKNAPP*. OVER THE NEXT THREE-AND-A-HALF SEASONS, DESPITE HIS POPULARITY WITH THE FANS AND HIS SUPERIOR GOALS-PER-MINUTE RATIO, *"SUPER PAV"* INVARIABLY FOUND HIMSELF DOWN THE PECKING ORDER BEHIND *ROBBIE KEANE*, *PETER CROUCH* AND *JERMAIN DEFOE*. BY EARLY 2012, HE WAS BACK IN RUSSIA WITH *LOKOMOTIV MOSCOW*.

IDENTIFY THESE OTHER PLAYERS SIGNED TO *TOTTENHAM HOTSPUR* DURING THE 12-MONTH TENURE OF *JUANDE RAMOS*:

1 FORMER *REAL MADRID* CENTRAL DEFENDER SIGNED FROM *MIDDLESBROUGH* FOR £8 MILLION.

2 DEFENDER SIGNED FROM GERMANY'S *HERTHA BSC*, THE FIRST BRAZILIAN TO PLAY FOR *TOTTENHAM'S* FIRST-TEAM. THE MOVE FAILED BADLY AND WHEN HIS CONTRACT WAS TERMINATED BY MUTUAL CONSENT IN JULY, 2009, HE RETURNED TO BRAZIL.

3 CAPPED 50 TIMES BY *SCOTLAND*, HE WAS A £9 MILLION BUY FROM *RANGERS* WHO WAS A FOOTBALL LEAGUE CUP WINNER IN ONLY HIS THIRD APPEARANCE FOR *TOTTENHAM*.

4 SIGNED FROM *DINAMO ZAGREB* FOR £16.5 MILLION, A SLIGHT MIDFIELDER WHO WOULD INSPIRE *SPURS* TO A FIRST EUROPEAN CUP/CHAMPIONS LEAGUE CAMPAIGN IN HALF A CENTURY.

5 *CROATIA* DEFENDER SIGNED FROM *MANCHESTER CITY* IN AN £8.5 MILLION DEAL.

6 STRIKER SIGNED FROM *MANCHESTER UNITED* ON LOAN AS PART OF THE DEAL THAT TOOK *DIMITAR BERBATOV* TO *OLD TRAFFORD*.

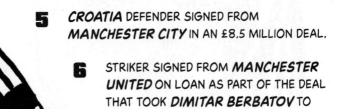

DIVE STATIONS!

JÜRGEN KLINSMANN ARRIVED AT *WHITE HART LANE* IN 1994 AS A GENUINE WORLD CUP-WINNING SUPERSTAR WHO HAD SCORED GOALS AT THE HIGHEST LEVEL IN GERMANY, ITALY AND FRANCE. BUT THE 30-YEAR-OLD STRIKER HAD A REPUTATION FOR GOING DOWN EASILY ... AND ON HIS DEBUT FOR *SPURS* AWAY TO *SHEFFIELD WEDNESDAY*, HE WAS GREETED BY A CACOPHONY OF BOOS AND JEERS FROM AWAY FANS HOLDING UP DIVING SCORECARDS. WHEN HE SCORED WHAT WOULD PROVE TO BE THE GAME-WINNING GOAL, HE LED HIS TEAMMATES IN AN EXAGGERATED DIVING ROUTINE IN CELEBRATION. THE SELF-DEPRECATING GESTURE MADE HIM AN INSTANT HERO TO THE *TOTTENHAM* FAITHFUL!

KLINSMANN WAS A MEMBER OF THE *WEST GERMANY* TEAM THAT WON THE FIFA WORLD CUP IN 1990. IDENTIFY THESE OTHER PAST, PRESENT OR FUTURE *TOTTENHAM* PLAYERS WHO PARTICIPATED IN ITALIA '90:

1 ITALIAN MIDFIELDER WHO JOINED *SPURS* IN 1998 AFTER A DECADE WITH *INTERNAZIONALE* DURING WHICH HE WON TWO UEFA CUPS.

2 *ENGLAND* WINGER WHO HAD LEFT *SPURS* TO JOIN *MARSEILLE* THE PREVIOUS YEAR.

3 *SCOTLAND* STRIKER WHO WOULD LEAVE *STAMFORD BRIDGE* FOR *WHITE HART LANE* THE FOLLOWING YEAR.

4 BELGIAN STRIKER WHO HAD SPENT TWO YEARS WITH *TOTTENHAM* AFTER IMPRESSING IN THE PREVIOUS WORLD CUP TOURNAMENT.

5 STRIKER WHO HAD WON THE GOLDEN BOOT AT THE 1986 WORLD CUP.

6 GOALKEEPER WHO REPRESENTED THE *UNITED STATES* IN FOUR WORLD CUP TOURNAMENTS.

7 SWEDISH-BORN *SCOTLAND* DEFENDER WHO HAD CAPTAINED *SPURS* IN THE 1987 FA CUP FINAL.

8 THE FIRST MIXED RACE PLAYER TO PLAY FOR THE *REPUBLIC OF IRELAND*, HE WOULD LEAVE *SPURS* FOR *WEST HAM* LATER THAT YEAR AFTER 13 YEARS AT *WHITE HART LANE*.

9 *ROMANIA* STRIKER WHO WOULD JOIN *TOTTENHAM* AFTER IMPRESSIVE FORM AT THE 1994 WORLD CUP.

THE PRINCE

ALTHOUGH BORN IN GERMANY, *KEVIN-PRINCE BOATENG* ELECTED TO REPRESENT *GHANA* AT INTERNATIONAL LEVEL -- UNLIKE HIS HALF-BROTHER *JÉRÔME BOATENG,* WHO WON THE WORLD CUP WITH GERMANY IN 2014.

1 *KEVIN-PRINCE BOATENG* JOINED *SPURS* FROM *HERTHA BSC* IN THE SUMMER OF 2007 -- WHO WAS THE MANAGER WHO SIGNED HIM?

2 HE WAS LOANED OUT TO *BORUSSIA DORTMUND* IN JANUARY OF 2009 -- WHO WAS THE *TOTTENHAM* MANAGER AT THE TIME?

3 WHO WAS *BOATENG'S* MANAGER AT *BORUSSIA DORTMUND?*

4 WHO WAS THE MANAGER WHO SIGNED *BOATENG* TO *PORTSMOUTH* IN THE SUMMER OF 2009?

5 IN THE 2010 FA CUP FINAL BETWEEN *PORTSMOUTH* AND *CHELSEA,* WHICH PLAYER WAS RULED OUT OF THE IMPENDING WORLD CUP FOLLOWING A RECKLESS *BOATENG* CHALLENGE IN RETALIATION FOR BEING SLAPPED?

6 WITH WHICH TEAM DID *BOATENG* WIN A SERIE A TITLE IN 2011?

7 HE HAD TWO SEASONS AT *SCHALKE 04* BETWEEN 2013 AND 2015, WHERE HE PLAYED UNDER WHICH FORMER *CHELSEA* MANAGER?

8 PLAYING UNDER MANAGER *NIKO KOVAČ,* WITH WHICH GERMAN CLUB DID *BOATENG* WIN THE DFB-POKAL IN 2018?

9 PLAYING ON LOAN FOR COACH *ERNESTO VALVERDE,* WITH WHICH TEAM DID *BOATENG* WIN LA LIGA IN 2019?

10 FOR WHICH TURKISH TEAM DID *BOATENG* PLAY IN 2020?

THE CENTURIONS

SIGNED FROM *PSV EINDHOVEN* IN 2005, *LEE YOUNG-PYO* WON A LEAGUE CUP MEDAL WITH *SPURS* BEFORE MOVING ON TO *BORUSSIA DORTMUND* IN 2008, THE YEAR HE BECAME THE SEVENTH *SOUTH KOREA* PLAYER TO EARN 100 CAPS. HE WAS EVENTUALLY CAPPED 127 TIMES.

NAME THESE OTHER *SPURS* CENTURIONS:

1 146 CAPS: *REPUBLIC OF IRELAND* 1998-2016

2 141 CAPS: *UNITED STATES* 2004-2017

3 119 CAPS: *NORTHERN IRELAND* 1964-1986

4 115 CAPS: *MOROCCO* 1990-2006

5 109 CAPS: *DENMARK* 2010-2021

6 109 CAPS: *NETHERLANDS* 2001-2013

7 108 CAPS: *WEST GERMANY/GERMANY* 1987-1998

8 107 CAPS: *MEXICO* 2007-2018

9 103 CAPS: *CROATIA* 2006-2018

10 102 CAPS: *UNITED STATES* 1990-2007

MEET THE NEW BOSS, SAME AS THE OLD BOSS

TERRY FENWICK PLAYED UNDER MANAGER **TERRY VENABLES** AT **CRYSTAL PALACE, QUEENS PARK RANGERS** AND **TOTTENHAM.**

THE FOLLOWING PLAYERS WORKED UNDER WHICH MANAGERS WITH MULTIPLE TEAMS?

1 PAT JENNINGS -- SPURS, ARSENAL

2 PETER CROUCH -- SOUTHAMPTON, PORTSMOUTH, SPURS

3 GARY LINEKER -- BARCELONA, SPURS

4 DEAN RICHARDS -- SOUTHAMPTON, SPURS

5 JERMAIN DEFOE - WEST HAM, PORTSMOUTH, SPURS

6 WILLIE YOUNG -- SPURS, ARSENAL

7 CLIVE WILSON -- QPR, SPURS

8 DARREN ANDERTON -- SPURS, WOLVES

9 DIMITAR BERBATOV -- FULHAM, SPURS

10 NIKO KRANJČAR -- PORTSMOUTH, SPURS, QPR

LILYWHITE RED MEN

A GOALSCORING STRIKER WITH **BLACKPOOL** AND **MANCHESTER CITY**, £1.7 MILLION SIGNING **PAUL STEWART** WAS CONVERTED TO A MIDFIELDER DURING HIS TIME AT **SPURS**, TURNING IN A GOALSCORING, MAN OF THE MATCH PERFORMANCE IN THE 1991 FA CUP FINAL TRIUMPH. HE JOINED **LIVERPOOL** THE FOLLOWING YEAR IN A £2.3 MILLION TRANSFER.

IDENTIFY THESE OTHERS WHO PLAYED FOR **SPURS** AND **LIVERPOOL**:

1 AGGRESSIVE, CONTROVERSIAL CENTRAL DEFENDER WHO JOINED **LIVERPOOL** FROM **TOTTENHAM** IN A £2.5 MILLION DEAL IN 1993, HE LATER PLAYED FOR **QPR**, **WEST HAM UNITED**, **CRYSTAL PALACE**, **SWINDON TOWN** AND MORE.

2 IRISH STRIKER WHO LEFT **TOTTENHAM** IN 2008 FOR **LIVERPOOL** FOR £19 MILLION PLUS £1.3 MILLION IN POTENTIAL ADD-ONS ... BUT WAS BACK AT **SPURS** A LITTLE OVER SIX MONTHS LATER!

3 FORWARD CAPPED 60 TIMES BY **ISRAEL**, HE JOINED **TOTTENHAM** FROM **LIVERPOOL** IN EARLY 1994. AFTER SCORING JUST 4 GOALS IN 88 APPEARANCES, HE DROPPED DOWN TWO DIVISIONS TO END HIS PLAYING DAYS WITH **WATFORD**.

4 CAPPED 86 TIMES BY **NORWAY**, HE PLAYED FOR **WIMBLEDON**, **LIVERPOOL**, **SPURS** AND **ASTON VILLA** BETWEEN 1994 AND 2003 BEFORE RETURNING TO NORWAY TO JOIN **LYN**.

"MUSSELBURGH"

ONE OF THE MOST INVENTIVE NICKNAMES IN FOOTBALL WAS BESTOWED ON **JUSTIN EDINBURGH,** THE LEFT-BACK WHO WON FA CUP AND LEAGUE CUP HONOURS WITH **SPURS** IN THE '90S. MUSSELBURGH IS A TOWN THAT LIES FIVE MILES OUTSIDE SCOTLAND'S CAPITAL CITY ... SO POETIC LICENCE DICTATED THAT **"MUSSELBURGH"** IS **JUST IN EDINBURGH!**

FOLLOWING HIS DECADE WITH *TOTTENHAM*, *EDINBURGH* SPENT
THREE SEASONS AT *PORTSMOUTH* BEFORE GOING INTO MANAGEMENT.
IDENTIFY THESE OTHER *SPURS* ALUMNI WITH *PORTSMOUTH* LINKS:

1 STRIKER WHO HAD TWO SPELLS WITH *SPURS* AND TWO WITH
PORTSMOUTH IN A CAREER THAT TOOK HIM TO *QPR*, *ASTON
VILLA*, *NORWICH*, *SOUTHAMPTON*, *LIVERPOOL*, *STOKE* AND
BURNLEY AND THE 2006 AND 2010 WORLD CUPS WITH *ENGLAND*.

2 A PREMIER LEAGUE WINNER WITH *BLACKBURN ROVERS*, HE SPENT
FIVE SEASONS WITH *TOTTENHAM* AND WON PROMOTION WITH
PORTSMOUTH AND LATER MANAGED *SPURS* AND *ASTON VILLA*.

3 FRENCH CENTRE-BACK WHO LEFT *SPURS* FOR *PORTSMOUTH* IN
2008, RETURNED TO *TOTTENHAM* TWO YEARS LATER, WHERE HIS
SIX SEASONS BROUGHT A LEAGUE CUP MEDAL, BEFORE HE MOVED
ON TO *SUNDERLAND* AND *WATFORD*.

4 GOALKEEPER WHO ROSE THROUGH FOUR DIVISIONS WITH
WIMBLEDON AND CAPTAINED THE 1988 FA CUP-WINNING TEAM,
BEFORE HIS TRAVELS TOOK HIM TO MORE THAN A DOZEN CLUBS,
INCLUDING *SPURS* AND TWO STINTS WITH *PORTSMOUTH*.

5 *ENGLAND* MIDFIELDER WHO SPENT A DOZEN SEASONS WITH
TOTTENHAM AFTER SIGNING FROM *PORTSMOUTH* IN A £1.75
MILLION DEAL IN 1992. HE LATER PLAYED FOR *BIRMINGHAM CITY*,
WOLVES AND *BOURNEMOUTH*.

6 EIGHT SEASONS WITH *FULHAM* BROUGHT PROMOTION IN 2001 AND
THE INTERTOTO CUP IN 2002, BEFORE HE HAD TWO INJURY-PLAGUED
SEASONS AT *TOTTENHAM*. HE WON THE FA CUP WITH *"POMPEY"*
IN 2008 AND LATER PLAYED FOR *BOLTON* AND *BRISTOL CITY*.

7 HE FOLLOWED HIS FIVE SEASONS AT *SPURS* WITH FOUR WITH
MANCHESTER UNITED, DURING WHICH TIME HE WON A PLETHORA
OF HONOURS, INCLUDING A HISTORIC TREBLE IN 1999, BEFORE
RETURNING TO *TOTTENHAM* IN 2001. HE LATER PLAYED FOR
PORTSMOUTH, *WEST HAM* AND MORE.

8 *CROATIA* INTERNATIONAL WHO WON THE 2008 FA CUP WITH
PORTSMOUTH BEFORE SPENDING THREE SEASONS AT *SPURS*.

THE LANE AND THE BRIDGE

A THIGH INJURY HE RECEIVED SERVING AS A CAPTAIN IN THE BRITISH ARMY DURING THE FIRST WORLD WAR ENDED **VIVIAN WOODWARD'S** CAREER IN TOP-FLIGHT FOOTBALL. THE 29 GOALS THAT HE SCORED IN 23 GAMES BETWEEN 1903 AND 1911 WAS AN **ENGLAND** RECORD THAT STOOD FOR 47 YEARS. HE ALSO PLAYED FOR **ENGLAND AMATEURS**, FOR WHOM HE SCORED 57 GOALS IN 44 GAMES, AND CAPTAINED **GREAT BRITAIN** TO GOLD MEDALS AT THE OLYMPIC GAMES OF 1908 AND 1912. AT CLUB LEVEL, HE SPENT EIGHT YEARS WITH **TOTTENHAM** -- HE SCORED THE CLUB'S FIRST EVER GOAL IN THE FOOTBALL LEAGUE IN SEPTEMBER 1908 -- BEFORE JOINING **CHELSEA** IN 1909.

IDENTIFY THESE OTHERS WHO HAVE PLAYED FOR **SPURS** AND **CHELSEA**:

1 **URUGUAY** INTERNATIONAL WHO WON FA CUP AND UEFA CUP HONOURS WITH **CHELSEA** BEFORE JOINING **SPURS** IN 2001. HE WAS SUBSEQUENTLY **TOTTENHAM** ASSISTANT MANAGER BEFORE TAKING THE REINS AT **BRIGHTON, SUNDERLAND** AND MORE.

2 SECOND DIVISION WINNER WITH **CHELSEA** IN 1989, **SCOTLAND** STRIKER WHO SCORED **TOTTENHAM'S** FIRST PREMIER LEAGUE GOAL, HE LATER WON MULTIPLE HONOURS WITH **RANGERS**.

3 MIDFIELDER WHO PLAYED FOR **CHELSEA, SPURS, QPR** AND **CRYSTAL PALACE** BEFORE EMBARKING ON THE MANAGEMENT CAREER THAT SAW HIM MANAGE THREE OF THOSE FOUR CLUBS AS WELL AS TWO NATIONAL TEAMS AND MORE.

4 BURLY **ENGLAND** STRIKER WHO LAUNCHED HIS CAREER AT **CHELSEA** AND WAS **TOTTENHAM'S** LEADING GOALSCORER IN THE 1960-61 DOUBLE-WINNING SEASON WITH 33 GOALS IN 43 GAMES.

5 ITALIAN WHO WAS **CHELSEA'S** FIRST-CHOICE GOALKEEPER UNTIL THE ARRIVAL OF **PETR ČECH**, HE WAS SUBSEQUENTLY BACK-UP AT **TOTTENHAM** BEFORE JOINING **LA GALAXY** IN 2012.

6 SIGNED FROM **CHELSEA**, HE WAS A DOUBLE-WINNER WITH **SPURS** IN 1961 AND LATER JOINED **QPR**. HIS SON, **CLIVE**, ALSO PLAYED FOR ALL THREE CLUBS AND BOTH WERE **ENGLAND** INTERNATIONALS.

7 MIDFIELDER WHO WON HIS FIRST FOUR *ENGLAND* CAPS WHILE PLAYING FOR FOUR DIFFERENT CLUBS -- *CHARLTON ATHLETIC, CHELSEA, NEWCASTLE UNITED* AND *WEST HAM UNITED* -- SPENT TWO SEASONS WITH *SPURS* BEFORE JOINING *FULHAM*, A TEAM HE LATER MANAGED BEFORE TAKING THE REINS AT *BOURNEMOUTH*.

8 CAPPED SIX TIMES BY *ENGLAND*, HE CAPTAINED THE 1984 UEFA CUP-WINNING TEAM, WON LEAGUE AND CUP HONOURS WITH *RANGERS* AND WAS A SECOND DIVISION WINNER WITH *CHELSEA* IN 1989.

9 1984 UEFA CUP WINNER WITH *SPURS*, HE WAS BRIEFLY LOANED OUT TO *CHELSEA* AND WENT ON TO PLAY FOR *WATFORD, RANGERS, QPR* AND *MILLWALL*.

10 *SCOTLAND* GOALKEEPER WHO PLAYED FOR A NUMBER OF CLUBS, INCLUDING *WIMBLEDON, TOTTENHAM, CHELSEA* AND *LEEDS UNITED*, AND WON A NUMBER OF HONOURS WITH *DONCASTER ROVERS* IN SEVEN SEASONS WITH THE CLUB BETWEEN 2006 AND 2013.

GAZZA!

PAUL GASCOIGNE OVERCAME CHILDHOOD POVERTY, DEPRIVATION AND ADVERSITY TO BECOME A WORLD SUPERSTAR ... BUT SADLY, WHEN HIS PLAYING DAYS WERE OVER, HIS STRUGGLES WITH ALCOHOL, HIS TROUBLED MENTAL WELL-BEING AND HIS LEGAL WOES ACCELERATED GREATLY.

1 PAUL GASCOIGNE LAUNCHED HIS CAREER AT NEWCASTLE UNITED -- NAME THE TWO MANAGERS UNDER WHOM HE PLAYED BETWEEN HIS 1985 DEBUT AND 1988 DEPARTURE.

2 WHO WAS THE MANAGER WHO SIGNED GASCOIGNE TO SPURS IN A BRITISH RECORD £2.2 MILLION DEAL IN 1988?

3 IN HIS FIRST SEASON WITH TOTTENHAM, HE SCORED FOUR GOALS IN A 5-0 LEAGUE CUP SECOND ROUND THRASHING OF WHICH TEAM?

4 GAZZA BECAME A HOUSEHOLD NAME PLAYING FOR BOBBY ROBSON'S ENGLAND AT ITALIA '90. NAME THE THREE OTHER ENGLAND MANAGERS UNDER WHOM PAUL GASCOIGNE PLAYED.

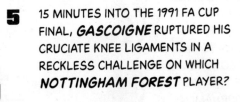

5 15 MINUTES INTO THE 1991 FA CUP FINAL, GASCOIGNE RUPTURED HIS CRUCIATE KNEE LIGAMENTS IN A RECKLESS CHALLENGE ON WHICH NOTTINGHAM FOREST PLAYER?

6 HE WAS OUT FOR A FULL YEAR BEFORE JOINING LAZIO IN 1992 -- WHICH WORLD CUP GREAT WAS MANAGER OF LAZIO AT THAT TIME?

7 WHO WAS THE MANAGER WHO SIGNED GASCOIGNE TO RANGERS IN 1995?

8 WHICH FORMER ENGLAND TEAMMATE WAS THE MANAGER WHO SIGNED GASCOIGNE TO MIDDLESBROUGH IN 1998?

9 GASCOIGNE BROKE HIS ARM ELBOWING WHICH ASTON VILLA PLAYER IN THE HEAD, AND EARNED HIMSELF A THREE-GAME BAN?

10 NAME ONE OF THE TWO CLUBS GASCOIGNE PLAYED FOR BETWEEN 2000 AND 2002 BEFORE LEAVING ENGLAND TO PLAY IN CHINA.

11 GASCOIGNE WAS APPOINTED MANAGER OF WHICH CONFERENCE NORTH CLUB IN 2005?

ENGLAND EXPECTS

GLENN HODDLE WAS CAPPED 53 TIMES BY **ENGLAND,** AND PLAYED IN THE 1982 AND 1986 WORLD CUPS. IN HIS THREE-YEAR TENURE AS **ENGLAND** MANAGER, HE STEERED THE TEAM TO THE SECOND ROUND OF THE 1998 TOURNAMENT.

NAME THESE OTHER *TOTTENHAM* PLAYERS CAPPED BY *ENGLAND:*

1 80 CAPS 1984-1992: FIFA WORLD CUP GOLDEN BOOT WINNER IN 1986

2 75 CAPS 2008-2017: FOUR TIMES PREMIER LEAGUE GOLDEN GLOVE WINNER WHO HAS PLAYED IN ENGLAND, SCOTLAND AND ITALY

3 73 CAPS 1996-2007: DEFENDER WHO WON HONOURS WITH *TOTTENHAM HOTSPUR, ARSENAL* AND *PORTSMOUTH*

4 67 CAPS 1966-1974: A WORLD CUP WINNER IN HIS EIGHTH APPEARANCE FOR *ENGLAND*

5 62 CAPS 1985-1991: CAPPED WHILE PLAYING FOR *NEWCASTLE UNITED, SPURS* AND *MARSEILLE*

6 61 CAPS 1972-1983: THREE-TIMES CHAMPIONS LEAGUE-WINNING GOALKEEPER WHO KEPT 460 CLEAN SHEETS DURING HIS CAREER

7 57 CAPS 1959-1967: SCORED 44 GOALS FOR *ENGLAND*

8 57 CAPS 1988-1998: BBC SPORTS PERSONALITY OF THE YEAR IN 1990

9 57 CAPS 2004-2017: 20 GOAL STRIKER WHO WON HIS CAPS WHILE PLAYING FOR *SPURS, PORTSMOUTH* AND *SUNDERLAND*

10 51 CAPS 1993-2002: FORWARD NAMED PFA PLAYERS' PLAYER OF THE YEAR AND FWA FOOTBALLER OF THE YEAR IN 2001

11 42 CAPS 2005-2010: SCORED 22 GOALS WHILE PLAYING FOR *SOUTHAMPTON, LIVERPOOL, PORTSMOUTH* AND *SPURS*

12 41 CAPS 2003-2007: GOALKEEPER WHO PLAYED FOR *LEEDS UNITED, SPURS, BLACKBURN ROVERS* AND *BURNLEY*

13 35 CAPS 1964-1971: THE FIRST *ENGLAND* PLAYER EVER SENT OFF IN A FULL INTERNATIONAL MATCH

14 34 CAPS 2001-2015: MIDFIELDER WHO HIS CAPS WHILE PLAYING FOR *WEST HAM UNITED, SPURS* AND *MANCHESTER UNITED*

ALF'S WINGLESS WONDERS

AS A **TOTTENHAM** PLAYER, **ALF RAMSEY** -- CAPPED 32 TIMES BY **ENGLAND** -- FOLLOWED HIS SECOND DIVISION TITLE WITH THE LEAGUE TITLE THE FOLLOWING SEASON. MOVING INTO MANAGEMENT, HE ACHIEVED THE SAME FEAT WITH **IPSWICH TOWN** BEFORE STEERING HIS **ENGLAND** TEAM OF "WINGLESS WONDERS" TO WORLD CUP GLORY IN 1966.

WHICH FORMER **SPURS** PLAYER MANAGED THE NATIONAL TEAM OF:

1   **PAKISTAN** (2010-11), **NEPAL** (2011-12)

2   **INDIA** (1984), **NEPAL** (1987)

3   **WALES** (1988-93), **LEBANON** (1995-97)

4   **GERMANY** (2004-06), **UNITED STATES** (2011-16)

5   **ENGLAND** (1994-96), **AUSTRALIA** (1997-98)

6   **TRINIDAD & TOBAGO** (2000)

7   **WALES** (1980-88)

8   **QATAR** (1994-97)

9   **NORTHERN IRELAND** (1976-79)

10   **BAHRAIN** (2011-12)

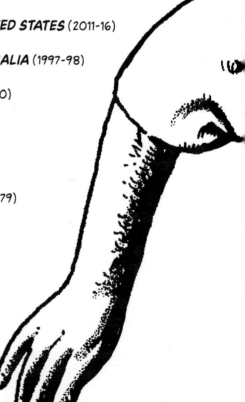

THE PITBULL

NICKNAMED *"THE PITBULL"* BY *LOUIS VAN GAAL* FOR HIS AGGRESSIVE AND TENACIOUS TACKLING, *EDGAR DAVIDS* -- WHO PLAYED IN GOGGLES DUE TO HIS GLAUCOMA -- WAS CAPPED 74 TIMES BY THE *NETHERLANDS.*

1 WITH WHICH CLUB DID *DAVIDS* WIN THREE LEAGUE TITLES, THE 1992 UEFA CUP AND THE 1995 UEFA CHAMPIONS LEAGUE?

2 HE SPENT 18 MONTHS AT WHICH ITALIAN CLUB, WHERE HIS MANAGERS INCLUDED *FABIO CAPELLO, ÓSCAR TABÁREZ* AND *ARRIGO SACCHI* AND TEAMMATES INCLUDED *FRANCO BARESI, GEORGE WEAH* AND *MARCEL DESAILLY?*

3 BETWEEN 1998 AND 2004, *DAVIDS* WON THREE LEAGUE TITLES WITH WHICH CLUB, WHERE HE PLAYED ALONGSIDE *ZINEDINE ZIDANE?*

4 DURING A LOAN SPELL WITH *BARCELONA*, HE PLAYED UNDER WHICH MANAGER, A FORMER *NETHERLANDS* TEAMMATE?

5 HE PLAYED FOR WHICH ITALIAN CLUB FOR ONE SEASON BEFORE JOINING *SPURS* ON A FREE TRANSFER IN 2006?

6 *DAVIDS* SPENT TWO SEASONS AT *TOTTENHAM HOTSPUR* PLAYING UNDER WHICH MANAGER?

7 NAME THE FIVE MANAGERS UNDER WHOM HE PLAYED FOR THE *NETHERLANDS* BETWEEN 1994 AND 2005?

8 IN 2010, *DAVIDS* SPENT A BRIEF PERIOD PLAYING FOR WHICH CHAMPIONSHIP TEAM?

9 IN 2012, *EDGAR DAVIDS* BECAME PLAYER/MANAGER OF WHICH LEAGUE TWO TEAM?

10 IN 2021, HE BRIEFLY MANAGED *OLHANENSE*, A TEAM PLAYING IN THE LOWER LEAGUES OF WHICH COUNTRY?

THE SPECIAL ONE

THE FIRST COACH TO SPEND MORE THAN £1 BILLION ON TRANSFERS, *JOSÉ MOURINHO* HAD WON MULTIPLE HONOURS WITH *PORTO, CHELSEA, INTERNAZIONALE, REAL MADRID* AND *MANCHESTER UNITED* -- INCLUDING EIGHT LEAGUE TITLES, TWO UEFA CHAMPIONS LEAGUES, THE UEFA CUP AND THE EUROPA LEAGUE -- BEFORE TAKING THE REINS AT *SPURS* IN LATE 2019. HE WAS DISMISSED SEVENTEEN MONTHS LATER, JUST DAYS BEFORE THE FOOTBALL LEAGUE CUP FINAL AGAINST *MANCHESTER CITY.* IT WAS THE FIRST TIME HE HAD LEFT A CLUB WITHOUT WINNING A TROPHY SINCE 2002.

FROM WHICH CLUBS DID THE FOLLOWING JOIN *TOTTENHAM* DURING *MOURINHO'S* TENURE?

1 GIOVANI LO CELSO

2 STEVEN BERGWIJN

3 SERGIO REGUILÓN

4 MATT DOHERTY

5 PIERRE-EMILE HÖJBJERG

6 JOE RODON

7 GEDSON FERNANDES

8 CARLOS VINÍCIUS

9 GARETH BALE

10 JOE HART

SAINTLY BOYS

GRZEGORZ RASIAK, THE TALL AND RANGY STRIKER CAPPED 37 TIMES BY **POLAND**, PLAYED FOR SIX CLUBS DURING HIS SIX YEARS IN ENGLISH FOOTBALL. HE SCORED 18 GOALS FOR **DERBY COUNTY** IN HIS DEBUT SEASON IN 2004 BUT FINANCIAL PRESSURES FORCED **"THE RAMS"** TO SELL HIM. FOLLOWING HIS £3 MILLION TRANSFER TO **SPURS**, HE FOUND IT DIFFICULT TO BREAK INTO THE FIRST TEAM AND HE WAS LOANED OUT TO **SOUTHAMPTON** IN EARLY 2006, THE MOVE BECOMING PERMANENT THAT SUMMER. HIS PROLIFIC 19-GOAL START TO THE 2007-2008 SEASON PETERED OUT AND LOAN MOVES TO **BOLTON WANDERERS** AND **WATFORD** WERE FOLLOWED BY A TRANSFER TO **READING** IN 2009. A YEAR LATER, HE JOINED **AEL LIMASSOL** OF CYPRUS ON A FREE TRANSFER, BUT THE MOVE ENDED IN ACRIMONY AND HE RETURNED TO HIS NATIVE POLAND TO SEE OUT HIS PLAYING CAREER.

IDENTIFY THESE OTHER **SPURS** PLAYERS WITH **SOUTHAMPTON** LINKS:

1 **KENYA** INTERNATIONAL MIDFIELDER WHO WON LEAGUE AND CUP HONOURS WITH **CELTIC**, HE SPENT THREE SEASONS WITH **"THE SAINTS"** BEFORE JOINING **SPURS** IN AN £11 MILLION DEAL IN 2016. HE WAS TRANSFERRED TO MLS SIDE **MONTREAL IMPACT (NOW CF MONTRÉAL)** IN 2020.

2 NICKNAMED **"RAZOR"**, HE PLAYED FOR **MILLWALL** AND **SOUTHAMPTON** IN BETWEEN TWO SPELLS AT **SPURS**, BEFORE SIGNING FOR **LIVERPOOL** FOR £2.5 MILLION IN 2003.

3 **ENGLAND** INTERNATIONAL RIGHT-BACK WHO SUBSEQUENTLY MANAGED THE NATIONAL TEAM, HE JOINED **SPURS** FROM **SOUTHAMPTON** IN 1949, GOING ON TO WIN SECOND AND FIRST DIVISION TITLES.

4 A FIFA U-20 WORLD CUP WINNER WITH **ENGLAND** IN 2017, HE SPENT THE EARLY YEARS OF HIS CAREER WITH **TOTTENHAM** BEFORE A LOAN MOVE TO **SOUTHAMPTON** WAS MADE PERMANENT IN 2020.

5 HAVING PLAYED IN THE SECOND TIER WITH **BRADFORD CITY** AND **WOLVES**, HE WAS AN £8.1 MILLION SIGNING TO **SPURS** FROM **SOUTHAMPTON** IN 2001. HE DIED AT THE AGE OF 36 IN 2011.

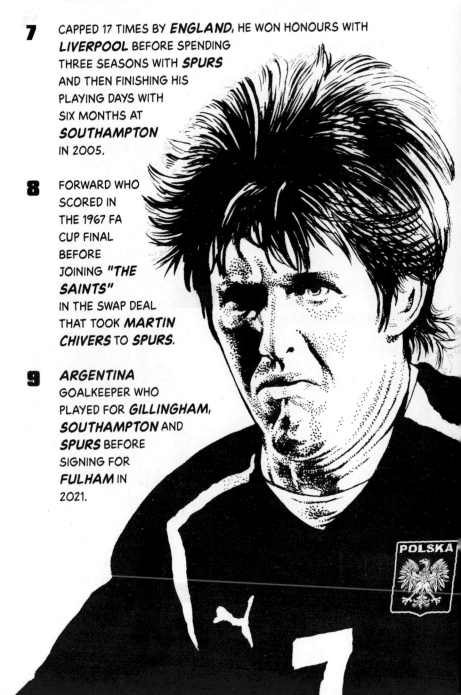

6 GOALKEEPER CAPPED 102 TIMES BY THE *U.S.*, HIS CLUBS INCLUDED *MILLWALL, LEICESTER CITY, SPURS, SOUTHAMPTON* AND *FULHAM* AS WELL AS TEAMS IN GERMANY, SPAIN AND THE STATES.

7 CAPPED 17 TIMES BY *ENGLAND*, HE WON HONOURS WITH *LIVERPOOL* BEFORE SPENDING THREE SEASONS WITH *SPURS* AND THEN FINISHING HIS PLAYING DAYS WITH SIX MONTHS AT *SOUTHAMPTON* IN 2005.

8 FORWARD WHO SCORED IN THE 1967 FA CUP FINAL BEFORE JOINING *"THE SAINTS"* IN THE SWAP DEAL THAT TOOK *MARTIN CHIVERS* TO *SPURS*.

9 *ARGENTINA* GOALKEEPER WHO PLAYED FOR *GILLINGHAM, SOUTHAMPTON* AND *SPURS* BEFORE SIGNING FOR *FULHAM* IN 2021.

GUNNERS TAKE CHARGE

THROUGHOUT **TOTTENHAM'S** HISTORY, THE CLUB HAS BEEN MANAGED BY A NUMBER OF MEN WHO PLAYED FOR ARCH RIVALS **ARSENAL. BILLY MINTER** AND **CLIVE ALLEN** PLAYED FOR BOTH TEAMS ... BUT **WALLY HARDINGE, JOE HULME, TERRY NEILL** AND **GEORGE GRAHAM** WERE ALL FORMER **ARSENAL** MEN WHO HAD NEVER PLAYED FOR **SPURS. NEILL** AND **GRAHAM** ARE UNIQUE IN THAT THEY MANAGED BOTH **ARSENAL** AND **TOTTENHAM.**

FROM WHICH TEAMS WERE THE FOLLOWING PLAYERS SIGNED DURING **GEORGE GRAHAM'S** TENURE AT THE CLUB?

1   SERGIY REBROV

2   BEN THATCHER

3   TIM SHERWOOD

4   CHRIS PERRY

5   ÖYVIND LEONHARDSEN

6   WILLEM KORSTEN

7   GARY DOHERTY

8   ANTHONY GARDNER

9   STEFFEN FREUND

10   SIMON DAVIES

11   MATTHEW ETHERINGTON

12   STEVEN FERGUSON

13   NEIL SULLIVAN

14   YANNICK KAMANAN

15   ANDY BOOTH

16   ROGER NILSEN

TOTTENHAM'S WORLD CUP GOALGETTERS

ENGLAND'S LEADING GOALSCORER AT WORLD CUP TOURNAMENTS IS ***GARY LINEKER***, WHO FOUND THE NET 10 TIMES OVER THE TWO TOURNAMENTS IN WHICH HE PARTICIPATED. HIS SIX GOALS AT THE 1986 WORLD CUP EARNED HIM THE GOLDEN BOOT, AND HE FOLLOWED UP WITH FOUR MORE AT ITALIA '90.

IDENTIFY THESE OTHER ***TOTTENHAM*** PLAYERS -- PAST, PRESENT AND FUTURE -- WHO SCORED FOR ***ENGLAND*** AT THE WORLD CUP.

1 1962: ***ARGENTINA***

2 1966: ***WEST GERMANY***   1970: ***WEST GERMANY***

3 1970: ***WEST GERMANY***

4 1998: ***COLOMBIA***

5 2002: ***SWEDEN***

6 2006: ***TRINIDAD AND TOBAGO***

7 2010: ***SLOVENIA***

8 2018: ***SWEDEN***

9 2018: ***PANAMA*** (3), ***TUNISIA*** (2), ***COLOMBIA***

10 2018: ***CROATIA***

NICE ONE, CYRIL ...

"NICE ONE, CYRIL" WAS A SONG WITH WHICH *SPURS* FANS REGALED LEFT-BACK *CYRIL KNOWLES*. IT WAS ADAPTED FROM AN AD FOR *WONDERLOAF* BREAD CREATED BY *"A YEAR IN PROVENCE"* AUTHOR *PETER MAYLE* IN HIS ADVERTISING EXECUTIVE DAYS. SIGNED FROM *MIDDLESBROUGH* IN 1964, *KNOWLES* WON MULTIPLE HONOURS IN HIS 11 YEARS WITH *TOTTENHAM*, INCLUDING THE FA CUP, THE UEFA CUP AND TWO LEAGUE CUPS. HE WENT ON TO MANAGE *DARLINGTON* AND *TORQUAY UNITED* AND WAS IN CHARGE OF *HARTLEPOOL UNITED* WHEN HE WAS DIAGNOSED WITH WHAT PROVED TO BE A FATAL BRAIN TUMOUR AT THE AGE OF 47 IN 1991.

WHICH FORMER *TOTTENHAM HOTSPUR* PLAYER'S MANAGEMENT CAREER INCLUDES SPELLS IN CHARGE OF:

1 1992-2012: *ENFIELD, YEOVIL TOWN, CHESHAM UNITED, HERTFORD TOWN, BOREHAM WOOD, CARSHALTON ATHLETIC, BRAINTREE TOWN, CLYDE, PAKISTAN, NEPAL*

2 1976-1997: *BRIGHTON & HOVE ALBION, CHARLTON ATHLETIC, CRYSTAL PALACE, ATM FA, BARNET*

3 1997-: *NEWCASTLE UNITED, BIRMINGHAM CITY, NORWICH CITY, BRIGHTON & HOVE ALBION, NOTTINGHAM FOREST*

4 1983-2014: *INDIA, NEPAL, DONCASTER ROVERS, WIMBLEDON, LUTON TOWN, NOTTINGHAM FOREST, NEWCASTLE UNITED*

5 1986-2009: *SWANSEA CITY, WALES, BRADFORD CITY, CARDIFF CITY, LEBANON, SHEFFIELD WEDNESDAY, MARGATE*

6 1995-: *PORTSMOUTH, NORTHAMPTON TOWN, SAN JUAN JABLOTEH, CENTRAL FC, C.S. VISÉ, TRINIDAD & TOBAGO*

7 2006-: *BRIGHTON & HOVE ALBION, SUNDERLAND, AEK ATHENS, BETIS, SHANGHAI SHENHUA, BORDEAUX, UNIVERSIDAD CATÓLICA*

THE WILLIE HALL HAUL

IN THE 7-0 THRASHING OF **NORTHERN IRELAND** ON NOVEMBER 16, 1938, **TOTTENHAM'S WILLIE HALL** SCORED **FIVE** OF **ENGLAND'S** GOALS -- THREE OF THEM IN JUST 3 MINUTES AND 30 SECONDS, SETTING A RECORD FOR THE FASTEST HAT-TRICK IN INTERNATIONAL FOOTBALL HISTORY THAT STOOD FOR ANOTHER 62 YEARS!

IDENTIFY THESE **ENGLAND** RECORDS SET BY ERSTWHILE **TOTTENHAM HOTSPUR** PLAYERS :

1 WHICH STRIKER HIT THREE GOALS OR MORE IN ONE GAME FOR **ENGLAND** SIX TIMES BETWEEN 1960 AND 1966?

2 WITH HIS GOAL IN A 2-2 DRAW WITH **GREECE** IN 2001, AT THE AGE OF 35 YEARS AND 187 DAYS, WHO BECAME **ENGLAND'S** OLDEST GOALSCORER IN A WORLD CUP QUALIFYING MATCH?

3 **HARRY KANE'S** SIX GOALS IN THE 2018 WORLD CUP MATCHED **GARY LINEKER'S** TALLY IN WHICH WORLD CUP TOURNAMENT?

4 WITH HIS FOUR GOALS AGAINST **MALAYSIA** IN 1991, WHO BECAME THE OLDEST PLAYER TO SCORE A HAT-TRICK FOR **ENGLAND**, AT THE AGE OF 30 YEARS AND 194 DAYS?

5 WHO WAS THE FIRST **TOTTENHAM** PLAYER TO REPRESENT **ENGLAND** AT THREE WORLD CUPS AND THREE EUROPEAN CHAMPIONSHIPS?

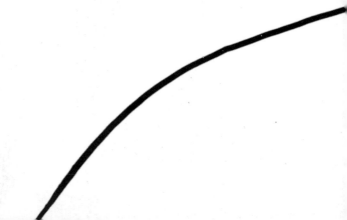

THE BOYS OF '81

TOTTENHAM AND **MANCHESTER CITY** CONTESTED THE 100TH FA CUP FINAL IN 1981. THE GAME ENDED IN A 1-1 DRAW AND WAS REPLAYED FIVE DAYS LATER, THE FIRST REPLAY SINCE 1970 AND THE FIRST EVER STAGED AT WEMBLEY. **SPURS** RAN OUT 3-2 WINNERS, THE FIVE GOALS MAKING THE GAME THE HIGHEST SCORING FA CUP FINAL REPLAY.

WHICH CLUBS DID THESE MEMBERS OF THE 1981 **SPURS** TEAM JOIN NEXT?

1	MILIJA ALEKSIC	**7**	OSVALDO ARDILES
2	CHRIS HUGHTON	**8**	STEVE ARCHIBALD
3	PAUL MILLER	**9**	TONY GALVIN
4	GRAHAM ROBERTS	**10**	GLENN HODDLE
5	STEVE PERRYMAN	**11**	GARTH CROOKS
6	RICARDO VILLA	**12**	GARRY BROOKE

KEEP IT CLEAN!

IN HIS 1,118-GAME CAREER, *RAY CLEMENCE* KEPT A RECORD 460 CLEAN SHEETS! HAVING LAUNCHED HIS CAREER AT *SCUNTHORPE UNITED*, DURING HIS 14 YEARS AT *LIVERPOOL* AND HIS SEVEN WITH *SPURS*, HIS MEDAL HAUL INCLUDED THREE EUROPEAN CUPS, FIVE LEAGUE TITLES, THREE UEFA CUPS, A UEFA SUPER CUP, TWO FA CUPS AND A LEAGUE CUP.

CLEMENCE SERVED AS JOINT MANGER OF *SPURS*, IN TANDEM WITH *DOUG LIVERMORE*, IN THE EARLY 1990S. IDENTIFY THESE *TOTTENHAM* MANAGERS BY THE EUROPEAN TROPHIES THEY WON AS PLAYERS:

1 UEFA CUP 1972 AND 1984 WITH *TOTTENHAM*

2 1970 INTER-CITIES FAIRS CUP WITH *ARSENAL*

3 1984 UEFA CUP WITH *SPURS* BEFORE JOINING *MONACO*

4 1984 UEFA CUP WITH *SPURS* BEFORE JOINING *WEST HAM*

5 UEFA CUP IN 2003 AND CHAMPIONS LEAGUE 2004 WITH *PORTO*

6 1984 UEFA CUP WITH *SPURS* BEFORE JOINING *BLACKBURN ROVERS*

THE MIDFIELD DYNAMO

HAVING WON MULTIPLE HONOURS WITH **BAYERN MUNICH**, DANISH
INTERNATIONAL **PIERRE-EMILE HØJBJERG** JOINED **SOUTHAMPTON**
IN 2016. HIS STELLAR PERFORMANCES IN MIDFIELD FOR **"THE SAINTS"**
PERSUADED **TOTTENHAM** TO SHELL OUT £15 MILLION PLUS ADD-ONS
IN 2020. IN HIS DEBUT SEASON, HE RACKED UP A LUNG-BUSTING 3,420
MINUTES TO LEAD THE PREMIER LEAGUE IN MINUTES PLAYED -- BUT HE
COULDN'T HELP **TOTTENHAM** WIN A TROPHY, **SPURS** GOING DOWN 1-0
TO **MANCHESTER CITY** IN THE LEAGUE CUP FINAL.

FROM WHICH CLUBS WERE THESE OTHER MEMBERS OF THAT 2021 LEAGUE
CUP FINAL SQUAD RECRUITED?

1 *HUGO LLORIS*

2 *SERGE AURIER*

3 *TOBY ALDERWEIRELD*

4 *ERIC DIER*

5 *SERGIO REGUILÓN*

6 *LUCAS MOURA*

7 *GIOVANI LO CELSO*

8 *SON HEUNG-MIN*

9 *JOE HART*

10 *DAVINSON SÁNCHEZ*

11 *ERIK LAMELA*

12 *MOUSSA SISSOKO*

13 *DELE ALLI*

14 *TANGUY NDOMBELE*

15 *GARETH BALE*

16 *STEVEN BERGWIJN*

TEAM MEMBERS *HARRY WINKS, HARRY KANE* AND *JAPHET TANGANGA* ALL CAME THROUGH THE RANKS AT *SPURS.*

THE ICEMAN COMETH

WHEN **TOTTENHAM** SIGNED **DIMITAR BERBATOV** FROM **BAYER LEVERKUSEN** IN 2006, HE BECAME THE FIRST BULGARIAN TO PLAY IN THE PREMIER LEAGUE. **BULGARIA'S** ALL-TIME LEADING GOALSCORER, HE WON THE 2008 LEAGUE CUP DURING HIS THREE SEASONS WITH **SPURS**.

BERBATOV WAS A **MARTIN JOL** SIGNING. FROM WHICH CLUBS WERE THE FOLLOWING PLAYERS SIGNED DURING THE DUTCHMAN'S TENURE?

1 **DARREN BENT**

2 **JERMAINE JENAS**

3 **GARETH BALE**

4 **DIDIER ZOKORA**

5 **YOUNÈS KABOUL**

6 **PASCAL CHIMBONDA**

7 **ANDY REID**

8 **KEVIN-PRINCE BOATENG**

9 **MICHAEL DAWSON**

10 **MIDO**

11 **BENOÎT ASSOU-EKOTTO**

12 **RICARDO ROCHA**

13 **TOM HUDDLESTONE**

14 **ADEL TAARABT**

"THE DELSTROYER"

SIGNED TO *MAURICIO POCHETTINO'S TOTTENHAM* FROM *MILTON KEYNES DONS* IN FEBRUARY 2015, *DELE ALLI* WAS LOANED BACK TO THE CLUB FOR THE REMAINDER OF THE SEASON -- AND DULY HELPED *MK DONS* WIN PROMOTION TO THE CHAMPIONSHIP, EARNING HIMSELF THE FOOTBALL LEAGUE YOUNG PLAYER OF THE YEAR AWARD IN THE PROCESS. IN HIS DEBUT SEASON WITH *SPURS*, HE WON THE FIRST OF HIS TWO CONSECUTIVE PFA YOUNG PLAYER OF THE YEAR AWARDS.

FROM WHICH CLUBS WERE THE FOLLOWING PLAYERS SIGNED DURING *POCHETTINO'S* TENURE AT *TOTTENHAM?*

1 *TANGUY NDOMBÉLÉ*

2 *DAVINSON SÁNCHEZ*

3 *MOUSSA SISSOKO*

4 *HEUNG-MIN SON*

5 *LUCAS MOURA*

6 *RYAN SESSEGNON*

7 *SERGE AURIER*

8 *VINCENT JANSSEN*

9 *TOBY ALDERWEIRELD*

10 *GIOVANI LO CELSO*

11 *FERNANDO LLORENTE*

12 *VICTOR WANYAMA*

13 *CLINTON N'JIE*

14 *GEORGES-KEVIN N'KOUDOU*

15 BEN DAVIES

16 JUAN FOYTH

17 JACK CLARKE

18 FEDERICO FAZIO

19 KEVIN WIMMER

20 BENJAMIN STAMBOULI

21 MICHEL VORM

22 ERIC DIER

23 KIERAN TRIPPIER

24 DEANDRE YEDLIN

OSSIE! OSSIE! OSSIE!

A WORLD CUP WINNER WITH *ARGENTINA* IN 1978, *OSSIE ARDILES* WON MULTIPLE HONOURS WITH *SPURS* AND PLAYED FOR CLUBS IN ENGLAND, FRANCE AND THE UNITED STATES BEFORE EMBARKING ON THE MANAGEMENT CAREER THAT SAW HIM TAKE CHARGE OF 15 DIFFERENT TEAMS IN ENGLAND, MEXICO, CROATIA, JAPAN, SYRIA, SAUDI ARABIA, MALAYSIA, PARAGUAY AND HIS NATIVE ARGENTINA.

IDENTIFY THESE CLUBS *OSSIE ARDILES* EITHER PLAYED FOR BY THE MANAGERS HE PLAYED UNDER ... OR MANAGED BY THE TIME FRAME AND THE MANAGER HE SUCCEEDED:

1 1998 PLAYED UNDER: *ROY HODGSON*

2 1998-99 PLAYED UNDER: *JIM SMITH*

3 MANAGED, 1989-1991: SUCCEEDED *LOU MACARI*

4 MANAGED, 1991-1992: SUCCEEDED *BOBBY SAXTON*

5 MANAGED, 1992-1993: SUCCEEDED *BOBBY GOULD*

6 MANAGED, 1993-1994: SUCCEEDED *DOUG LIVERMORE* AND *RAY CLEMENCE*

THE OLD FIRM

CAPPED 75 TIMES BY *ENGLAND*, *JOE HART* WON FOUR PREMIER LEAGUE GOLDEN GLOVES, TWO LEAGUE TITLES AND FOUR DOMESTIC CUPS WHILE AT *MANCHESTER CITY*. THE ARRIVAL OF *PEP GUARDIOLA* MEANT THE END OF *HART'S* TIME AT *CITY* AND HE SUBSEQUENTLY BOUNCED FROM CLUB TO CLUB, WITH SPELLS AT *TORINO*, *WEST HAM*, *BURNLEY* AND *TOTTENHAM*, BEFORE SIGNING FOR *CELTIC* IN SUMMER 2021.

IDENTIFY THESE PLAYERS WITH LINKS TO **SPURS** AND A GLASGOW CLUB:

1 *USA* INTERNATIONAL CENTRE-BACK WHO FOLLOWED LOANS AT **SHEFFIELD UNITED, IPSWICH TOWN, SWANSEA CITY, STOKE CITY, LUTON TOWN** AND **BOURNEMOUTH** BY SIGNING A LOAN DEAL WITH **CELTIC** FOR THE 2021-2022 SEASON.

2 *SWITZERLAND* CENTRE-BACK, A 1999 LEAGUE CUP WINNER WITH **SPURS**, HE WON THE TREBLE OF LEAGUE AND BOTH SCOTTISH CUPS ON LOAN AT CELTIC IN 2000-01 BEFORE JOINING **WATFORD**.

3 FAN FAVOURITE WINGER SIGNED TO **SPURS** FROM **RANGERS** IN 1974 -- THE LAST SIGNING MADE BY **BILL NICHOLSON** -- HE RETURNED TO SCOTLAND TO JOIN **CELTIC** IN 1977.

4 CROATIAN MIDFIELDER WHO PLAYED UNDER **HARRY REDKNAPP** AT THREE CLUBS, HE ENDED HIS CAREER WITH TWO SEASONS AT **RANGERS** BEFORE RETIRING IN 2018.

5 HAVING PLAYED FOR **CELTIC, CARLISLE UNITED** AND **SPURS**, HE WAS ASSISTANT TO **GLENN HODDLE** AT **SWINDON TOWN, ENGLAND** AND **SPURS**, AS WELL AS MANAGING IN HIS OWN RIGHT.

6 *ENGLAND* STRIKER WHO HAS PLAYED FOR **WEST HAM, BOURNEMOUTH, SPURS, PORTSMOUTH, TORONTO, SUNDERLAND, BOURNEMOUTH** AND MADE HIS **RANGERS** LOAN PERMANENT IN 2020.

7 *KENYA* MIDFIELDER WHO WON TWO LEAGUE TITLES IN HIS TWO SEASONS WITH **CELTIC**, HE JOINED **TOTTENHAM** FROM **SOUTHAMPTON** IN 2016.

8 A RECORD SIGNING FOR **SPURS** IN 1988, **ENGLAND** INTERNATIONAL MIDFIELDER WHO FOLLOWED A SPELL IN ITALY BY SIGNING FOR **RANGERS** IN 1995.

9 HAVING WON TWO FA CUPS AND THE UEFA CUP WITH **SPURS** IN THE EARLY 1980S, HE WON LEAGUE AND CUP HONOURS WITH **RANGERS**, BEFORE HELPING **CHELSEA** WIN PROMOTION IN 1989.

10 ALL-TIME **REPUBLIC OF IRELAND** LEADING GOALSCORER.

FROM NORTH LONDON TO THE FAR EAST

CAPPED 56 TIMES BY *BRAZIL*, WHEN HE REPRESENTED HIS COUNTRY AT THE 2014 WORLD CUP *PAULINHO* WAS A *TOTTENHAM* PLAYER ... AND WHEN HE PLAYED AT THE 2018 TOURNAMENT, HE WAS A LA LIGA WINNER WITH *BARCELONA*. IN BETWEEN, HE HAD SPENT THE FIRST OF HIS TWO SPELLS IN CHINA WITH *GUANGZHOU EVERGRANDE*, WITH WHOM HE WON THREE CHINESE SUPER LEAGUES, THE CHINESE FA CUP, TWO CHINESE FA SUPERCUPS AND THE AFC CHAMPIONS LEAGUE.

NAME THESE *SPURS* PLAYERS WHO PLIED THEIR TRADE IN THE FAR EAST:

1 AFTER WINNING THE 1991 FA CUP WITH *SPURS*, *ENGLAND* INTERNATIONAL WHO ENDED HIS PLAYING DAYS WITH TWO SEASONS WITH JAPAN'S *NAGOYA GRAMPUS EIGHT*.

2 CAPPED 82 TIMES BY *BELGIUM*, HE JOINED *SPURS* FROM *FULHAM* IN 2012, LEAVING FOR THE CHINA LEAGUE TEAM *GUANGZHOU R&F* FOR A REPORTED £11 MILLION FEE SIX-AND-A-HALF YEARS LATER.

3 YOUNGER BROTHER OF A *SPURS* AND *ENGLAND* GREAT, HE PLAYED FOR *NEGERI SEMBILAN FA* IN MALAYSIA IN 1986, BEFORE HIS CAREER TOOK HIM TO *BARNET*, *LEYTON ORIENT* AND MORE.

4 CAPPED 57 TIMES BY *ENGLAND*, A WORLD CUP STAR WHO PLAYED IN ITALY AND SCOTLAND AND IN 2003 HAD A BRIEF SPELL IN CHINA WITH *GANSU TIANMA*.

5 ICELANDIC STRIKER WHO WON LA LIGA AND A UEFA CHAMPIONS LEAGUE WITH *BARCELONA* AND TWO LEAGUE TITLES WITH *CHELSEA*, HE JOINED CHINESE SUPER LEAGUE SIDE *SHIJIAZHUANG EVER BRIGHT* IN 2015.

6 *WEST HAM* AND *SPURS* STRIKER, CAPPED 39 TIMES BY *MALI*, HE WON TWO UEFA CUPS WITH *SEVILLA* BEFORE JOINING CHINA'S *BEIJING GUOAN* IN 2012.

YANKEE DOODLE DEMPSEY

CAPPED 141 TIMES BY THE **UNITED STATES**, **CLINT DEMPSEY** IS TIED WITH **LANDON DONOVAN** AS THE COUNTRY'S ALL-TIME LEADING GOALSCORER ON 57 GOALS. **DEMPSEY** PLAYED IN FOUR CONCACAF GOLD CUPS -- WINNING THREE -- AND SCORED IN EACH OF THE THREE WORLD CUPS IN WHICH HE PARTICIPATED.

DEMPSEY WAS A £9 MILLION ACQUISITION FROM **FULHAM** IN 2012. NAME THESE OTHERS WHO PLAYED FOR BOTH **SPURS** AND **FULHAM:**

1 COMBATIVE MIDFIELDER WHO STARTED HIS CAREER AT **MANCHESTER CITY**, PLAYED FOR **SHEFFIELD UNITED**, **SPURS**, **FULHAM** AND **WIGAN ATHLETIC**, PLAYED IN AN FA CUP FINAL AND WAS RELEGATED WITH **PORTSMOUTH**, HAD THREE SEASONS WITH **LEEDS UNITED** AND THEN PLAYED FOR, AND SUBSEQUENTLY MANAGED, PORT VALE BEFORE BEING SACKED IN 2017.

2 **ENGLAND** MIDFIELDER WHO PLAYED FOR **CHELSEA**, **NEWCASTLE UNITED**, **WEST HAM**, **SPURS** AND **FULHAM** BEFORE GOING INTO MANAGEMENT WITH **FULHAM** IN 2019 BEFORE TAKING THE **BOURNEMOUTH** JOB IN 2020.

3 FRENCH MIDFIELDER WHO WON THE 2001 COUPE DE LA LIGUE WITH **LYON**, THE 2002 UEFA INTERTOTO CUP WITH **FULHAM**, AND THE 2008 LEAGUE CUP WITH **SPURS** BEFORE JOINING **SUNDERLAND**.

4 HAVING MADE HIS BREAKTHROUGH AT **FULHAM** AS A 16-YEAR-OLD HE WAS THE FIRST PLAYER BORN IN THE 2000S TO SCORE A GOAL IN THE ENGLISH PROFESSIONAL LEAGUES. HE JOINED **TOTTENHAM** IN A £25 MILLION DEAL IN 2019 AND WAS LOANED OUT TO **1899 HOFFENHEIM** THE FOLLOWING SEASON.

5 WINGER WHO WON THE DOUBLE IN 1961 AND THE EUROPEAN CUP WINNERS' CUP IN 1963, BEFORE LEAVING **SPURS** FOR **FULHAM**. HE LATER PLAYED FOR **COLCHESTER UNITED** AND **GUILDFORD CITY**.

6 **ENGLAND** MIDFIELDER WHO HAD TWO LENGTHY SPELLS WITH **FULHAM**, EITHER SIDE OF EIGHT YEARS WITH **SPURS**, DURING WHICH TIME HE WON THE 1967 FA CUP, THE 1971 LEAGUE CUP AND THE 1972 UEFA CUP.

SEMI-SKINNED

GARETH BALE JOINED *SPURS* IN THE SUMMER OF 2007. INJURY RULED HIM OUT OF THE SECOND HALF OF THE SEASON, WHICH MEANT THAT HE MISSED OUT ON AN FA CUP WINNER'S MEDAL. HE WAS A RUNNER-UP IN THE 2009 LEAGUE CUP FINAL AND WOULD GO ON TO PLAY ON THE LOSING SIDE IN TWO FA CUP SEMI-FINALS IN HIS FIRST SPELL AT THE CLUB. ON HIS SEASON-LONG RETURN AFTER WINNING MANY HONOURS WITH *REAL MADRID*, HE WAS ON THE LOSING SIDE IN THE 2021 LEAGUE CUP FINAL.

WHICH TEAM DEFEATED SPURS IN THESE SEMI-FINALS:

1   1921-22 FA CUP: LOST 2-1

2   1952-53 FA CUP: LOST 2-1

3   1955-56 FA CUP: LOST 1-0

4   1961-62 EUROPEAN CUP: LOST 4-3 ON AGGREGATE

5   1968-69 LEAGUE CUP: LOST 2-1 ON AGGREGATE

6   1971-72 LEAGUE CUP: LOST 4-5 ON AGGREGATE

7   1972-73 UEFA CUP: LOST ON AWAY GOALS AFTER 2-2 ON AGGREGATE

8   1975-76 LEAGUE CUP: LOST 3-2 ON AGGREGATE

9   1981-82 UEFA CUP WINNERS' CUP: LOST 2-1 ON AGGREGATE

10   1986-87 LEAGUE CUP: LOST REPLAY 2-1 AFTER 2-2 ON AGGREGATE

11   1991-92 LEAGUE CUP: LOST 3-2 ON AGGREGATE

12   1992-93 FA CUP: LOST 1-0

13   1994-95 FA CUP: LOST 4-1

14   1998-99 FA CUP: LOST 2-0

15 2000-01 FA CUP: LOST 2-1

16 2006-07 LEAGUE CUP: LOST 5-3 ON AGGREGATE

17 2009-10 FA CUP: LOST 2-0

18 2011-12 FA CUP: LOST 5-1

19 2016-17 FA CUP: LOST 4-2

20 2017-18 FA CUP: LOST 2-1

21 2018-19 LEAGUE CUP: LOST ON PENALTIES AFTER 2-2 ON AGGREGATE

MADRIDISTAS

ON LOAN AT REAL MADRID IN 2011, *EMMANUEL ADEBAYOR* EARNED A COPA DEL REY MEDAL WHEN *"LOS BLANCOS"* BEAT ARCH-RIVALS *BARCELONA* IN THE FINAL. YEARS LATER, THE *TOGO* STRIKER INSISTED THAT THE MOVE WAS NOT MADE PERMANENT BECAUSE HIS LATE BROTHER WROTE A LETTER TO THE SPANISH GIANTS ON BEHALF OF THE *ADEBAYOR* FAMILY URGING THE CLUB NOT TO SIGN HIM!

IDENTIFY THESE OTHERS WITH LINKS TO *SPURS* AND *REAL MADRID*:

1 HAVING WON LA LIGA WITH *REAL MADRID, SPAIN* STRIKER WHO JOINED *SPURS* IN A £26 MILLION DEAL IN 2013. AFTER AN UNDERWHELMING TWO-YEAR STAY, HE SUBSEQUENTLY PLAYED FOR *VILLARREAL, FENERBAHÇE, GRANADA* AND *LEVANTE.*

2 2010 WORLD CUP RUNNER-UP WITH THE *NETHERLANDS,* MIDFIELDER WHO WON HONOURS WITH *AJAX, HAMBURGER SV* AND *REAL MADRID* BEFORE JOINING *SPURS* IN 2010.

3 *CROATIA'S* MOST-CAPPED PLAYER, HE LEFT *SPURS* IN 2012 AFTER FOUR SEASONS FOR *REAL MADRID,* WITH WHOM HE HAS WON A PLETHORA OF HONOURS, INCLUDING FOUR CHAMPIONS LEAGUES.

4 *SPAIN* LEFT-BACK WHO JOINED *TOTTENHAM* FROM *REAL MADRID* IN 2020.

5 JOINED *REAL MADRID* FROM *TOTTENHAM* IN 2013 FOR A WORLD RECORD FEE OF £77 MILLION.

6 TWO-TIME CHAMPIONS LEAGUE-WINNING MANAGER WHO WON LEAGUE TITLES WITH *PORTO, CHELSEA, INTERNAZIONALE* AND *REAL MADRID* AND THE EUROPA LEAGUE AND FOOTBALL LEAGUE CUP WITH *MANCHESTER UNITED,* HE WAS IN CHARGE OF *TOTTENHAM* FOR 17 MONTHS.

7 CHAMPIONS LEAGUE-WINNING GOALKEEPER WITH *REAL MADRID* WHO JOINED *SPURS* IN 2008.

8   ENGLAND DEFENDER WHOSE CAREER PATH TOOK HIM FROM
LEEDS UNITED TO *NEWCASTLE UNITED, MIDDLESBROUGH,
TOTTENHAM, STOKE CITY* AND BACK TO *MIDDLESBROUGH.*

9   MANAGER SACKED BY *SPURS* IN OCTOBER, 2008 ... AND APPOINTED
BY *REAL MADRID* SIX WEEKS LATER.

CHARITY BEGINS AT HOME

TOTTENHAM'S FIRST APPEARANCE IN THE FA CHARITY SHIELD -- THE ANNUAL SEASON OPENER SINCE RENAMED THE FA COMMUNITY SHIELD -- WAS IN 1920, WHEN, AS SECOND DIVISION CHAMPIONS, THEY LOST 2-0 TO FIRST DIVISION CHAMPIONS **WEST BROMWICH ALBION.** THE NEXT YEAR, AS FA CUP WINNERS, THEY TOOK ON CHAMPIONS **BURNLEY,** WINNING 2-0 THROUGH GOALS BY **JIMMY CANTRELL** (LEFT) AND **BERT BLISS.** BOTH GAMES WERE PLAYED ON HOME SOIL AT **WHITE HART LANE.**

1   IN THE 1951 CHARITY SHIELD, REIGNING LEAGUE CHAMPIONS **TOTTENHAM** BEAT WHICH FA CUP HOLDERS 2-1?

2   IN 1961, BECAUSE THEY HAD WON THE LEAGUE AND FA CUP DOUBLE THE PREVIOUS SEASON, **SPURS** COMPETED FOR THE CHARITY SHIELD AGAINST A FOOTBALL ASSOCIATION REPRESENTATIVE TEAM. **SPURS** RAN OUT 3-2 WINNERS, WITH TWO OF THE GOALS SCORED BY WHICH INSIDE-FORWARD, WHOSE SON WOULD ALSO LATER PLAY FOR **TOTTENHAM HOTSPUR?**

3   THE 1962 CHARITY SHIELD GAME ENDED IN A 5-1 VICTORY FOR FA CUP HOLDERS **SPURS** OVER WHICH REIGNING LEAGUE CHAMPIONS?

4   THE 1967 CHARITY SHIELD GAME AGAINST LEAGUE CHAMPIONS **MANCHESTER UNITED** ENDED IN A 3-3 DRAW. **JIMMY ROBERTSON** AND **FRANK SAUL** SCORED FOR **TOTTENHAM** -- BUT WHO SCORED THE OTHER **SPURS** GOAL AND WHY WAS IT REMARKABLE?

5   THE 1981 CHARITY SHIELD PITTED THE FA CUP HOLDERS AGAINST REIGNING CHAMPIONS **ASTON VILLA.** **PETER WITHE** SCORED TWICE FOR **"THE VILLANS"** IN A 2-2 DRAW -- BUT WHICH STRIKER, WHO WOULD SUBSEQUENTLY PLAY FOR **CHELSEA, WATFORD, RANGERS, QUEENS PARK RANGERS** AND **MILLWALL,** SCORED A BRACE FOR **TOTTENHAM?**

6   THE 1982 CHARITY SHIELD ENDED IN A 1-0 LOSS TO WHICH REIGNING CHAMPIONS?

7   **TOTTENHAM'S** NEXT APPEARANCE IN A CHARITY SHIELD GAME CAME IN 1991 WHEN THEY DREW 0-0 WITH WHICH TEAM?

CARLING DARLINGS

THE FIRST LEAGUE CUP FINAL TO BE PLAYED AT THE NEW WEMBLEY STADIUM, THE 2008 FINAL ENDED IN A 2-1 WIN OVER CHELSEA. IT WAS TOTTENHAM'S FIRST TROPHY IN NINE YEARS AND SECURED A PLACE IN THE FOLLOWING SEASON'S UEFA CUP.

THE TEAM WAS CAPTAINED BY ONE-CLUB MAN *LEDLEY KING* ... BUT WHICH CLUB DID THESE MEMBERS OF THAT 2008 TEAM JOIN NEXT?

1 *PAUL ROBINSON*

2 *ALAN HUTTON*

3 *JONATHAN WOODGATE*

4 *PASCAL CHIMBONDA*

5 *AARON LENNON*

6 *JERMAINE JENAS*

7 *DIDIER ZOKORA*

8 *STEED MALBRANQUE*

9 *ROBBIE KEANE* (PICTURED RIGHT)

10 *DIMITAR BERBATOV*

11 *RADEK ČERNÝ*

12 *YOUNES KABOUL*

13 *TEEMU TAINIO*

14 *TOM HUDDLESTONE*

15 *DARREN BENT*

GONE TOO SOON?

IN 13 YEARS AT *TOTTENHAM*, *PAT JENNINGS* WON THE 1967 FA CUP, TWO LEAGUE CUPS AND THE 1972 UEFA CUP, AS WELL AS FWA AND PFA FOOTBALLER OF THE YEAR AWARDS. IN 1977, HE WAS ALLOWED TO JOIN *ARSENAL*, THE ASSUMPTION BEING THAT HE WAS NEARING THE END OF HIS CAREER. THE *NORTHERN IRELAND* GOALKEEPER HAD OTHER IDEAS -- IN HIS EIGHT YEARS AT *HIGHBURY*, HE HELPED *THE GUNNERS* REACH FOUR MAJOR FINALS, ADDING THE 1979 FA CUP TO HIS MEDAL TALLY.

IDENTIFY THESE OTHERS WHO PLAYED FOR *SPURS* AND *ARSENAL:*

1   FRENCH CENTRE-BACK WHO WON TWO LEAGUE TITLES AND THE LEAGUE CUP WITH *CHELSEA*, SPENT FOUR SEASONS WITH *ARSENAL* AND THEN JOINED *TOTTENHAM* IN 2010.

2   CAPTAIN OF *GREAT BRITAIN* AT THE 1960 OLYMPICS, A CENTRE-FORWARD WHO BECAME A CENTRE-HALF, HE PLAYED FOR *ARSENAL* FROM 1961 TO 1964, *SPURS* FROM 1964 TO 1966, JOINED *NORWICH CITY*, AND WAS PLAYER/ MANAGER WITH *BRADFORD PARK AVENUE* AND *ALTRINCHAM.*

3 TWO-TIME FA YOUTH CUP WINNER WITH **ARSENAL**, HE JOINED **SPURS** IN 2002. HIS SUBSEQUENT CAREER TOOK THE MIDFIELDER TO **COVENTRY**, **WOLVES**, **QPR**, **BARNSLEY** AND **EXETER CITY**, AND CLUBS IN CANADA, HUNGARY, MOLDOVA, GERMANY, IRELAND, INDIA, THAILAND, HONG KONG AND BANGLADESH.

4 CAPTAIN OF **TOTTENHAM'S** 1999 LEAGUE CUP-WINNING TEAM, AN **ENGLAND** CENTRE-HALF WHO WON MULTIPLE HONOURS WITH **ARSENAL**, INCLUDING THE LEAGUE AND FA CUP DOUBLE IN 2002, WON THE FA CUP WITH **PORTSMOUTH**, AND PLAYED FOR **NOTTS COUNTY** AND **NEWCASTLE UNITED**.

5 **ARSENAL** WINGER WHO WAS INJURED IN A COLLISION WITH **LEEDS UNITED** GOALKEEPER **GARY SPRAKE** IN THE 1968 LEAGUE CUP FINAL, HE JOINED **SPURS** IN A STRAIGHT SWAP FOR SCOTTISH WINGER **JIMMY ROBERTSON**.

6 SCOTTISH CENTRAL DEFENDER WHO LEFT **SPURS** FOR **ARSENAL** IN 1977, PLAYED IN THREE FA CUP FINALS -- WINNING IN 1979 -- AND PLAYED FOR **NOTTINGHAM FOREST**, **NORWICH CITY**, **BRIGHTON & HOVE ALBION** AND **DARLINGTON**.

AFRICA! AFRIQUE!

ALTHOUGH BORN AND RAISED IN FRANCE, **BENOÎT ASSOU-EKOTTO** OPTED TO REPRESENT **CAMEROON** AT INTERNATIONAL LEVEL. HE PARTICIPATED IN TWO WORLD CUPS, BUT HIS PARTICIPATION IN THE 2014 TOURNAMENT ENDED AFTER HE HEADBUTTED A TEAMMATE!

WHICH AFRICAN COUNTRIES HAVE THE FOLLOWING PLAYED FOR?

1 *VICTOR WANYAMA*

2 *EMMANUEL ADEBAYOR*

3 *KEVIN-PRINCE BOATENG*

4 *FRÉDÉRIC KANOUTÉ*

5 *NOUREDDINE NAYBET*

6 *SÉBASTIEN BASSONG*

7 *STEVEN PIENAAR*

8 *NABIL BENTALEB*

9 *DIDIER ZOKORA*

10 *JOHN CHIEDOZIE*

11 *CLINTON N'JIE*

12 *ADEL TAARABT*

13 *MOUSSA SAÏB*

14 *MBULELO MABIZELA*

15 *SERGE AURIER*

16 *MOUNIR EL HAMDAOUI*

BIG CHIV

WHEN **MARTIN CHIVERS** JOINED **TOTTENHAM HOTSPUR** FROM **SOUTHAMPTON** IN EARLY 1968, THE £125,000 FEE MADE HIM THE MOST EXPENSIVE BRITISH PLAYER AT THAT TIME. IN EIGHT SEASONS AT **WHITE HART LANE**, THE **ENGLAND** INTERNATIONAL WON TWO LEAGUE CUPS AND THE UEFA CUP, SCORING 174 GOALS IN 367 FIRST TEAM APPEARANCES. HE SUBSEQUENTLY PLAYED FOR **SERVETTE, NORWICH CITY, BRIGHTON & HOVE ALBION, DORCHESTER TOWN, FRANKSTON CITY, VARD HAUGESUND** AND **BARNET.**

CHIVERS GAINED HIS FIRST TROPHY WITH **SPURS** WHEN HE SCORED BOTH GOALS IN THE 2-0 WIN OVER **ASTON VILLA** IN THE 1971 LEAGUE CUP FINAL. WHO SCORED FOR **TOTTENHAM** IN THESE LEAGUE CUP FINALS?

1 1973 V **NORWICH CITY**
WON 1-0

2 1982 V **LIVERPOOL**
LOST 3-1

3 1999 V **LEICESTER CITY**
WON 1-0

4 2002 V **BLACKBURN ROVERS**
LOST 2-1

5 2008 V **CHELSEA**
WON 2-1

THE FORTUNATE SON

WINNING A GOLD MEDAL AT THE 2018 ASIAN GAMES MEANT THAT **SON HEUNG-MIN** AND HIS **SOUTH KOREA** TEAMMATES EARNED EXEMPTION FROM MANDATORY MILITARY SERVICE. THE FIRST ASIAN PLAYER IN HISTORY TO SCORE MORE THAN 50 GOALS IN THE PREMIER LEAGUE, HE IS CONSIDERED ONE OF THE GREATEST PLAYERS ASIA HAS EVER PRODUCED.

HE WAS NAMED **TOTTENHAM HOTSPUR** PLAYER OF THE YEAR IN 2018-19 AND 2019-20. IDENTIFY THESE OTHER WINNERS OF THE AWARD:.

1 NAME THE TWO BELGIAN INTERNATIONALS TO HAVE WON THE AWARD -- ONE IN 2015-16 AND THE OTHER IN 2017-18.

2 **ROBBIE KEANE** WON THE AWARD THREE TIMES -- CAN YOU NAME THE OTHER **REPUBLIC OF IRELAND** INTERNATIONAL WHO WON THE AWARD, HIS WINS COMING IN 1999 AND 2000?

3 IN 2002, WHO BECAME THE FIRST **WALES** INTERNATIONAL TO WIN?

4 CAN YOU NAME THE **NORWAY** INTERNATIONAL WHO WAS NAMED PLAYER OF THE YEAR IN 1989?

5 TO DATE, WHO IS THE ONLY **SCOTLAND** INTERNATIONAL TO WIN THE AWARD, HIS WIN COMING IN 2001?

THE HANDSOME ONE

NEEDING ONLY A DRAW IN THE FINAL GROUP GAME TO QUALIFY FOR THE 1994 WORLD CUP, WITH THE SCORE LEVEL AND JUST SECONDS TO GO, **PARIS SAINT-GERMAIN'S DAVID GINOLA** OVER-HIT A CROSS. **BULGARIA** TOOK POSSESSION, RACED DOWNFIELD AND SCORED THE WINNER, QUALIFYING AT **FRANCE'S** EXPENSE. **GÉRARD HOULLIER**, THE FRENCH TEAM MANAGER, BRANDED **GINOLA** "AN ASSASSIN". **GINOLA'S** EXPERIENCE IN ENGLISH FOOTBALL WAS MUCH HAPPIER. HE JOINED **SPURS** FROM **NEWCASTLE** IN 1997 AND WENT ON TO WIN THE 1999 LEAGUE CUP AND FWA FOOTBALLER OF THE YEAR AND PFA PLAYERS' PLAYER OF THE YEAR AWARDS.

GERRY FRANCIS WAS THE MANAGER WHO SIGNED **GINOLA**. FROM WHICH CLUBS WERE THESE PLAYERS ACQUIRED DURING THE **FRANCIS** ERA?

1 *LES FERDINAND*

2 *CHRIS ARMSTRONG*

3 *RUEL FOX*

4 *STEFFEN IVERSEN*

5 *JOHN SCALES*

6 *JOSÉ DOMINGUEZ*

7 *ALLAN NIELSEN*

8 *ANDY SINTON*

9 *CLIVE WILSON*

10 *ALAN PARDEW*

11 *RAMON VEGA*

THE REAL MACKAY

HAVING WON LEAGUE, CUP AND LEAGUE CUP HONOURS WITH **HEART OF MIDLOTHIAN**, 24-YEAR-OLD **DAVE MACKAY** JOINED **SPURS** IN 1959. BY THE TIME HE LEFT FOR **DERBY COUNTY** NINE YEARS LATER, HE HAD CARVED HIS NAME INTO **TOTTENHAM** LEGEND. ONE OF THE GREATEST MIDFIELDERS IN THE HISTORY OF THE CLUB, HIS MEDAL TALLY INCLUDED THE LEAGUE AND FA CUP DOUBLE, TWO FURTHER FA CUPS AND THE EUROPEAN CUP WINNERS' CUP.

IDENTIFY THESE OTHERS WHO PLAYED FOR **SPURS** AND **DERBY COUNTY:**

1 **NIGERIA** INTERNATIONAL WHO ESTABLISHED HIS REPUTATION AT **LEYTON ORIENT** AND **NOTTS COUNTY** BEFORE JOINING **SPURS** IN 1984. INJURIES DERAILED HIS MOMENTUM AND HE MOVED ON TO **DERBY COUNTY** IN 1988 AND BRIEFLY RETURNED TO **NOTTS COUNTY** TWO YEARS LATER.

2 **EGYPT** INTERNATIONAL WHO HAD A TORRID TIME AT **SPURS** AFTER HURLING HIS SHIRT TO THE GROUND AFTER BEING SUBSTITUTED, HE SPENT TIME ON LOAN AT **DERBY COUNTY** IN 2008.

3 ENGLAND MIDFIELDER WHO SPENT EIGHT SEASONS WITH **SPURS**, HAD TWO SPELLS AT **DERBY COUNTY** AND BEGAN HIS SECOND SPEl AT **HULL CITY** IN 2021.

4 **POLAND** STRIKER WHO JOINED **SPURS** FROM DERBY IN 2005 AND LATER PLAYED FOR **SOUTHAMPTON, BOLTON, WATFORD** AND MORE.

IMPORTED FROM PORTO

CAPPED 71 TIMES BY **PORTUGAL**, **HÉLDER POSTIGA** PLAYED HIS FOOTBALL IN PORTUGAL, SPAIN, GREECE, ENGLAND, FRANCE AND INDIA. **GLENN HODDLE** WAS THE MANAGER WHO BROUGHT HIM TO **SPURS** IN 2003 AFTER **POSTIGA** HAD WON A TREBLE WITH **PORTO** ... BUT HIS STAY WAS DISAPPOINTING AND HE WAS BACK WITH **PORTO** A YEAR LATER.

FROM WHICH CLUBS WERE THE FOLLOWING SIGNED DURING **GLENN HODDLE'S TOTTENHAM** TENURE?

1 DEAN RICHARDS

2 ROBBIE KEANE

3 CHRISTIAN ZIEGE

4 GORAN BUNJEVCEVIC

5 FRÉDÉRIC KANOUTÉ

6 GUSTAVO POYET

7 BOBBY ZAMORA

8 MILENKO ACIMOVIC

9 JONATHAN BLONDEL

10 TEDDY SHERINGHAM

11 JAMIE REDKNAPP

12 KASEY KELLER

13 ROHAN RICKETTS

14 PAUL KONCHESKY

15 DAVE BEASANT

16 *KAZUYUKI TODA*

17 *STÉPHANE DALMAT*

TOTALLY HAMMERED!

HIS IMPRESSIVE DISPLAYS FOR *ROMANIA* AT THE 1994 WORLD CUP EARNED *ILIE DUMITRESCU* A MOVE FROM *STEAUA BUCUREŞTI* TO *SPURS*. FOLLOWING A LOAN SPELL WITH *SEVILLA*, HE WAS SOLD TO *WEST HAM* IN 1996 -- BUT PROBLEMS WITH HIS WORK PERMIT MEANT THAT HE WAS SOON ON THE MOVE AGAIN, JOINING MEXICO'S *CLUB AMÉRICA*.

IDENTIFY THESE OTHERS WHO PLAYED FOR BOTH *SPURS* AND *WEST HAM UNITED:*

adidas

11

1 ARGENTINE FULL-BACK WHO SPENT FOUR YEARS AT *IPSWICH TOWN* BEFORE BECOMING *GEORGE GRAHAM'S* FIRST SIGNING TO *SPURS* IN 1998. SIX YEARS LATER, HE SIGNED FOR *WEST HAM* BUT TORE HIS HAMSTRING ON HIS DEBUT AND LEFT THE CLUB SOON AFTER BY MUTUAL CONSENT.

2 *TOTTENHAM* LEGEND WHO JOINED *WEST HAM UNITED* AS PART-EXCHANGE IN THE 1970 DEAL THAT TOOK *MARTIN PETERS* TO *WHITE HART LANE*, HE SCORED TWICE ON HIS HAMMERS DEBUT.

3 YOUTH STAR WITH *WEST HAM*, AN *ENGLAND* INTERNATIONAL WHO JOINED *SPURS* IN A £3.5 MILLION DEAL IN 2004. TWO YEARS LATER, *MANCHESTER UNITED* PAID £18 MILLION TO SIGN HIM. HE WENT ON TO BECOME ONE OF THE MOST DECORATED PLAYERS IN THE ENGLISH GAME AND AFTER 12 YEARS, ACCEPTED A COACHING ROLE AT *OLD TRAFFORD*.

4 *ENGLAND* MIDFIELDER WHO PLAYED FOR *CHARLTON ATHLETIC*, *NORWICH CITY*, *CHELSEA*, *NEWCASTLE UNITED*, *WEST HAM*, *SPURS* AND *FULHAM* BEFORE MOVING INTO MANAGEMENT WITH *FULHAM* AND *BOURNEMOUTH*.

5 *MALI* STRIKER WHO, AFTER SPELLS WITH *WEST HAM UNITED* AND *TOTTENHAM*, JOINED *SEVILLA* AND WON CONSECUTIVE UEFA CUPS IN 2006 AND 2007.

6 STRIKER WHO WON BACK-TO-BACK LOWER LEAGUE PROMOTIONS WITH *BRIGHTON & HOVE ALBION* BEFORE JOINING *SPURS* IN 2003. HE SIGNED FOR *WEST HAM* THE FOLLOWING YEAR AND SCORED THE PLAY-OFF-WINNING GOAL THAT TOOK THE *HAMMERS* BACK INTO THE TOP FLIGHT. FOUR SEASONS AT *FULHAM* WERE FOLLOWED BY A SWITCH TO *QUEENS PARK RANGERS* -- AND IN 2014, HE SCORED THE PLAY-OFF GOAL THAT TOOK *"THE HOOPS"* BACK INTO THE PREMIER LEAGUE AFTER A ONE-SEASON ABSENCE!

7 *ENGLAND* STRIKER WHOSE CLUBS INCLUDED *QPR*, *NEWCASTLE UNITED*, *SPURS*, *WEST HAM*, *LEICESTER*, *BOLTON WANDERERS*, *READING* AND *WATFORD* AND WHO WON A TURKISH CUP DURING A LOAN PERIOD WITH *BEŞIKTAŞ* IN 1989.

BOUNCING STRAIGHT BACK

A YOUNG *GLENN HODDLE* INSPIRED *TOTTENHAM HOTSPUR* TO SECURE A RETURN TO THE TOP FLIGHT AT THE FIRST ATTEMPT IN 1978, HAVING DROPPED OUT OF THE FIRST DIVISION THE PREVIOUS YEAR FOR THE FIRST TIME IN 27 SEASONS. *HODDLE* WENT ON TO BECOME A *SPURS* LEGEND, WINNING TWO FA CUPS AND THE UEFA CUP BEFORE JOINING *MONACO* IN 1987.

WHERE DID THESE OTHER MEMBERS OF THAT 1977-78 SQUAD GO NEXT?

1 *GERRY ARMSTRONG*

2 *RALPH COATES*

3 *BARRY DAINES*

4 *JOHN DUNCAN*

5 *JIMMY HOLMES*

6 *CHRIS JONES*

7 *COLIN LEE*

8 *DON MCALLISTER*

9 *NEIL MCNAB*

10 *IAN MOORES*

11 *TERRY NAYLOR*

12 *KEITH OSGOOD*

13 *STEVE PERRYMAN*

14 *JOHN PRATT*

15 *MARTIN ROBINSON*

16 MICKY STEAD

17 PETER TAYLOR

18 JOHN GORMAN

PLAYERS OF THE YEAR

A WORLDWIDE TV AUDIENCE WATCHED ON IN ANGUISH AND HORROR WHEN 29-YEAR-OLD *CHRISTIAN ERIKSEN* STAGGERED AND COLLAPSED DURING *DENMARK'S* OPENING GAME AGAINST *FINLAND* AT EURO 2020. CARDIOPULMONARY RESUSCITATION AND DEFIBRILLATION SUCCEEDED IN REVIVING HIM AND SAVING HIS LIFE. HE WAS DISCHARGED FROM HOSPITAL SIX DAYS LATER, HAVING HAD A CARDIOVERTER-DEFIBRILLATOR DEVICE IMPLANTED. FIVE TIMES DANISH FOOTBALLER OF THE YEAR, HE HAD WON HONOURS WITH *AJAX* AND REACHED TWO FINALS WITH *SPURS*, BEFORE WINNING THE 2021 SERIE A TITLE IN HIS DEBUT SEASON WITH *INTERNAZIONALE.*

IDENTIFY THESE OTHER PLAYER OF THE YEAR AWARD RECIPIENTS:

1 SEVEN TIMES BULGARIAN FOOTBALLER OF THE YEAR.

2 1993 FRENCH PLAYER OF THE YEAR AND BOTH PFA PLAYERS' PLAYER OF THE YEAR AND FWA FOOTBALLER OF THE YEAR IN 1999.

3 HIS 2020 CROATIAN FOOTBALLER OF THE YEAR AWARD WAS A RECORD-EXTENDING NINTH TIME HE HAD WON THE HONOUR.

4 GERMAN FOOTBALLER OF THE YEAR IN 1988 AND 1994.

5 2013 ROMANIAN FOOTBALLER OF THE YEAR.

6 NAME THE THREE *TOTTENHAM HOTSPUR* PLAYERS WHO HAVE WON U.S. SOCCER PLAYER OF THE YEAR AWARDS.

7 DUTCH EREDIVISIE FOOTBALLER OF THE YEAR IN 2012.

EVER-PRESENT PERRYMAN

STEVE PERRYMAN PLAYED IN 340 OF **TOTTENHAM'S** 344 LEAGUE GAMES BETWEEN AUGUST 1974 AND OCTOBER 1982 -- INCLUDING ONE RUN OF 173 CONSECUTIVE LEAGUE GAMES. HE ALSO MANAGED AT LEAST ONE GOAL IN EVERY ONE OF THE 17 SEASONS THAT SAW HIM MAKE A RECORD 854 APPEARANCES FOR THE CLUB.

IDENTIFY THESE OTHER TOTTENHAM HOTSPUR STALWARTS:

1 611 APPEARANCES 1982-1998: **ENGLAND** INTERNATIONAL MIDFIELDER SIGNED FROM **BRISTOL ROVERS**.

2 590 APPEARANCES 1964-1977: GOALKEEPER SIGNED FROM **WATFORD** WHO SUBSEQUENTLY PLAYED FOR **ARSENAL**.

3 523 APPEARANCES 1899-1912: FA CUP WINNER IN 1901, AFTER RETIRING, HE WAS A MEMBER OF THE GROUND STAFF UNTIL HIS 1942 DEATH.

4 506 APPEARANCES 1964-1975: **ENGLAND** LEFT-BACK SIGNED FROM **MIDDLESBROUGH**, HE LATER MANAGED **DARLINGTON**, **TORQUAY UNITED** AND **HARTLEPOOL UNITED**.

5 491 APPEARANCES 1975-1987: **TOTTENHAM** GREAT WHO LATER MANAGED **SPURS** AND **ENGLAND** AMONG OTHERS.

6 452 APPEARANCES 1946-1958: **ENGLAND** GOALKEEPER WHO LATER PLAYED FOR AND MANAGED **ROMFORD**.

7 439 APPEARANCES 1964-1974: **SCOTLAND** STRIKER SIGNED FROM **DUNDEE**, HE SCORED 133 GOALS FOR **SPURS**.

8 438 APPEARANCES 1919-1931: **ENGLAND** WINGER WHO SCORED THE WINNING GOAL IN THE 1921 FA CUP FINAL.

9 420 APPEARANCES 1963-1975: CENTRAL DEFENDER WHO WON 1971 AND 1973 LEAGUE CUPS AND 1972 UEFA CUP.

THE ITALIAN JOB

PAUL **GASCOIGNE** WAS ALL SET TO JOIN **LAZIO** FROM **SPURS** AT THE END OF THE 1990-91 SEASON UNTIL HE RUPTURED CRUCIATE LIGAMENTS PLAYING IN THE FA CUP FINAL AGAINST **NOTTINGHAM FOREST.** HE LOST AN ENTIRE SEASON RECOVERING FROM THE INJURY AND FINALLY JOINED THE ITALIANS IN THE SUMMER OF 1992.

WHICH ITALIAN CLUB DID THESE PLAYERS JOIN FROM *TOTTENHAM?*

1 *FEDERICO FAZIO* -- 2017

2 *CHRISTIAN ERIKSEN* -- 2020

3 *RODRIGO DEFENDI* -- 2007

4 *RETO ZIEGLER* -- 2007

5 *TONY MARCHI* -- 1957

6 *JOHNNY JORDAN* -- 1948

7 *VLAD CHIRICHEŞ* -- 2015

8 *FERNANDO LLORENTE* -- 2019

9 *IAGO FALQUE* -- 2014

FROM WHICH ITALIAN CLUB WERE THESE PLAYERS SIGNED TO *SPURS?*

10 *FERNANDO LLORENTE* -- 2013

11 *EDGAR DAVIDS* -- 2005

12 *NICOLA BERTI* -- 1998

13 *JIMMY GREAVES* -- 2013

14 *MIDO* -- 2006

MONIKERS!

NICKNAMES ARE UBIQUITOUS IN A DRESSING ROOM. SOME OF THEM ARE OBVIOUS AND SELF-EXPLANATORY -- *ROBBIE KEANE* WAS *"KEANO"*, *PAUL GASCOIGNE* WAS *"GAZZA"*, *STEVE ARCHIBALD* WAS *"ARCHIE"* AND *JIMMY GREAVES* WAS *"GREAVSIE"* -- BUT CAN YOU IDENTIFY THE FOLLOWING *SPURS* PLAYERS BY THEIR NICKNAMES?

1 THE RADIO

2 BILKO

3 ERIK THE VIKING

4 DEUCE

5 LONG NECK

6 THE GINGER PELÉ

7 JUKEBOX

8 GOLAZO

9 BROADWAY

10 ROCKET

11 SWEDE

12 THE RUSSIAN

13 TREACLE

14 MEATHOOK

15 MUSHY

16 WIPEY

17 ENO

18 DISCO BENNY

19 COCO

20 RAZOR

G-MAN GILLIE

A SCOTTISH LEAGUE CHAMPIONSHIP WINNER WITH *DUNDEE* IN 1962, *ALAN GILZEAN* HEADED SOUTH TO JOIN *SPURS* IN 1964, WHERE HE FORMED A SUCCESSFUL STRIKE PARTNERSHIP WITH *JIMMY GREAVES*, THE PAIR BEING DUBBED *"THE G-MEN"* BY THE FANS. *GILZEAN*, WHO WON THE FA CUP, TWO LEAGUE CUPS AND THE 1972 UEFA CUP IN HIS TIME AT *WHITE HART LANE*, ENDED HIS PLAYING DAYS WITH A THREE-MONTH SPELL IN SOUTH AFRICA WITH *HIGHLANDS PARK*.

IDENTIFY THESE OTHERS WITH SOUTH AFRICAN LINKS:

1 *SOUTH AFRICA* DEFENDER, HE WAS HIS COUNTRY'S YOUNGEST CAPTAIN AT THE AGE OF 22, WHICH EARNED HIM THE NICKNAME *"OLDJOHN"* -- INSPIRED BY HIS MOTHER'S MAIDEN NAME. HE JOINED SPURS FROM *ORLANDO PIRATES* IN 2003 AFTER CATCHING THE EYE DURING A *TOTTENHAM* SUMMER TOUR.

2 RIGHT-BACK WITH THE 1961 DOUBLE WINNERS, HE MADE 342 APPEARANCES FOR *TOTTENHAM* OVER 13 YEARS BEFORE EMIGRATING TO SOUTH AFRICA, WHERE HE PLAYED FOR -- AND LATER MANAGED -- *DURBAN UNITED*.

3 SWEDISH-BORN *SCOTLAND* INTERNATIONAL WHO WAS RAISED IN SOUTH AFRICA AND BEGAN HIS CAREER PLAYING WITH THE *WITS UNIVERSITY* CLUB.

4 HAVING PLAYED 364 GAMES FOR *FULHAM*, EITHER SIDE OF HIS 312 GAMES FOR *SPURS*, AND BEEN CAPPED 35 TIMES BY *ENGLAND*, HE ENDED HIS PLAYING DAYS IN 1976 WITH *DURBAN CITY*, BEFORE EMBARKING ON A MANAGEMENT CAREER THAT SAW HIM TAKE CHARGE OF *CHARLTON ATHLETIC, CRYSTAL PALACE* AND *QPR*, AS WELL AS TWO SPELLS WITH *BRIGHTON & HOVE ALBION*.

5 CAPPED 61 TIMES BY *SOUTH AFRICA* -- WITH WHOM HE PARTICIPATED IN THE 2002 AND 2010 WORLD CUPS -- HE WON HONOURS WITH *AJAX*, AND PLAYED FOR *SPURS, BORUSSIA DORTMUND* AND *SUNDERLAND*, BUT IS CHIEFLY REMEMBERED IN ENGLAND FOR HIS TWO SPELLS WITH *EVERTON*.

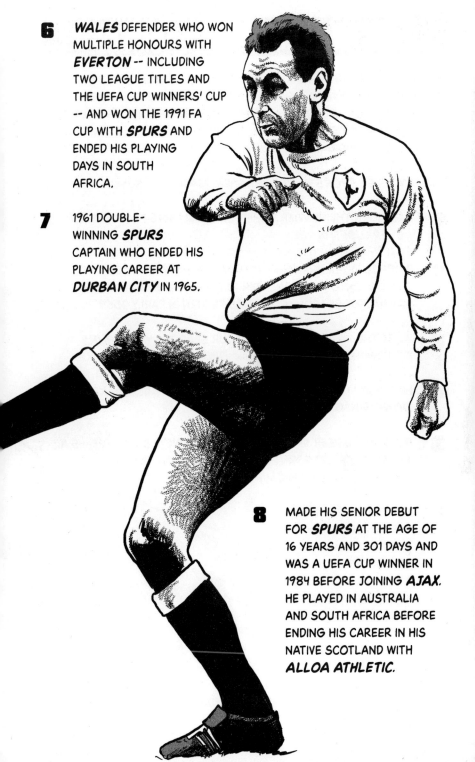

6 **WALES** DEFENDER WHO WON MULTIPLE HONOURS WITH **EVERTON** -- INCLUDING TWO LEAGUE TITLES AND THE UEFA CUP WINNERS' CUP -- AND WON THE 1991 FA CUP WITH **SPURS** AND ENDED HIS PLAYING DAYS IN SOUTH AFRICA.

7 1961 DOUBLE-WINNING **SPURS** CAPTAIN WHO ENDED HIS PLAYING CAREER AT **DURBAN CITY** IN 1965.

8 MADE HIS SENIOR DEBUT FOR **SPURS** AT THE AGE OF 16 YEARS AND 301 DAYS AND WAS A UEFA CUP WINNER IN 1984 BEFORE JOINING **AJAX.** HE PLAYED IN AUSTRALIA AND SOUTH AFRICA BEFORE ENDING HIS CAREER IN HIS NATIVE SCOTLAND WITH **ALLOA ATHLETIC.**

THE NUMBERS GAME

JAPHET TANGANGA HAS REPRESENTED *ENGLAND* AT EVERY YOUTH LEVEL FROM U-16 TO U-21, AND WAS A MEMBER OF THE TEAM THAT WON THE TOULON TOURNAMENT IN 2017. IN HIS BREAKTHROUGH SENIOR SEASON WITH *TOTTENHAM*, HE WORE THE NUMBER 39 SHIRT BUT HAS SUBSEQUENTLY WORN NUMBER 25.

IDENTIFY THESE *SPURS* PLAYERS BY THEIR TEAM SHIRT NUMBERS:

1 HAS WORN THE NUMBER 7 SHIRT SINCE ARRIVING FROM *BAYER 04 LEVERKUSEN* IN 2015.

2 WORE 22 AFTER ARRIVING FROM *LEEDS UNITED* IN 2002, HE SUBSEQUENTLY WORE NUMBER 10 IN HIS TWO SPELLS AT THE CLUB, BAR HALF-A-SEASON IN 15 ON HIS RETURN IN EARLY 2009.

3 WORE THE 14 SHIRT DURING HIS FOUR SEASONS WITH *SPURS* FOLLOWING HIS TRANSFER FROM *DINAMO ZAGREB* IN 2008.

4 HAS WORN NUMBER 20 SINCE ARRIVING FROM *MILTON KEYNES DONS* IN 2015.

5 HE WORE NUMBER 18 HIS ENTIRE TIME DURING HIS TWO SPELLS AT THE CLUB, EXCEPT FOR THE HALF-SEASON FOLLOWING HIS EARLY 2009 RETURN FROM *PORTSMOUTH*.

6 CONTINUES TO WEAR THE NUMBER 27 SHIRT HE TOOK FOLLOWING HIS TRANSFER FROM *PARIS SAINT-GERMAIN* IN EARLY 2018.

7 STRIKER WHO WORE THE NUMBER 15 SHIRT AT *SPURS*, *LIVERPOOL* AND *BURNLEY*, THE NUMBER 25 AT *STOKE CITY* AND *NORWICH CITY* AND VARIOUS NUMBERS AT HIS OTHER CLUBS.

8 MEXICAN WHO WORE 17 AT *SPURS*, *RACING SANTANDER* AND FOR SOME OF HIS TIME WITH *BARCELONA*.

9 CENTRAL MIDFIELDER WHO WORE 19 AT *SPURS* AND FOR MOST OF HIS APPEARANCES FOR BELGIUM, HAVING WORN THE NUMBER 30 FOR *FULHAM*.

WHEN **GARETH BALE** SCORED THREE GOALS IN THE 4-3 LOSS TO **INTERNAZIONALE** IN A UEFA CHAMPIONS LEAGUE GAME AT THE **SAN SIRO** IN 2010, IT WAS THE FIRST TIME A **SPURS** PLAYER HAD SCORED A HAT-TRICK AND FINISHED ON THE LOSING SIDE SINCE **FRANK OSBORNE** AGAINST **LEICESTER** IN 1925.

1 **BALE'S** CAREER HAS TAKEN HIM FROM **SOUTHAMPTON** TO **TOTTENHAM** AND ON TO **REAL MADRID**. NAME THREE OF THE MANAGERS UNDER WHOM HE HAS PLAYED AT THOSE CLUBS BETWEEN 2006 AND 2021.

2 NAME THREE **WALES** MANAGERS UNDER WHOM HE HAS PLAYED BETWEEN HIS 2006 DEBUT AND 2021.

OH, DANNY BOY ...

NORTHERN IRELAND MIDFIELDER **DANNY BLANCHFLOWER** WAS CAPPED 56 TIMES AND CAPTAINED HIS COUNTRY AT THE 1958 WORLD CUP. TWICE VOTED FWA FOOTBALLER OF THE YEAR, DURING HIS DECADE AT **WHITE HART LANE** HE CAPTAINED **SPURS** TO A LEAGUE AND FA CUP DOUBLE IN 1961 -- DURING WHICH HE PLAYED IN EVERY GAME OF THE SEASON -- THE FA CUP IN 1962 AND THE EUROPEAN CUP WINNERS' CUP IN 1963. HE RETIRED IN 1964, BRIEFLY PLAYED FOR **DURBAN CITY** IN 1965, THEN BECAME A RESPECTED JOURNALIST, AS WELL AS MANAGING **NORTHERN IRELAND** AND **CHELSEA**.

WHICH CLUB DID THE FOLLOWING MEMBERS OF THE SQUAD THAT WON THE DOUBLE IN 1961 JOIN AFTER LEAVING **TOTTENHAM?**

1 *BILL BROWN*

2 *PETER BAKER*

3 *DAVE MACKAY*

4 *CLIFF JONES*

5 *BOBBY SMITH*

6 *LES ALLEN*

7 *TERRY DYSON*

8 *FRANK SAUL*

TEAM MEMBERS **RON HENRY** AND **MAURICE NORMAN** RETIRED AFTER PLAYING FOR **SPURS**, **JOHN WHITE** DIED IN 1964.

THE BOYS OF '84

PLAYED OVER TWO LEGS, THE 1984 UEFA CUP FINAL ENDED ALL SQUARE AND WAS DECIDED ON A PENALTY SHOOT-OUT. IN WHAT WAS HIS LAST COMPETITIVE GAME FOR *TOTTENHAM* BEFORE JOINING *BARCELONA*, *SCOTLAND* STRIKER *STEVE ARCHIBALD* SCORED ONE OF THE DECISIVE PENALTY KICKS TO GIVE *SPURS* VICTORY OVER *ANDERLECHT*.

WHICH CLUBS DID THESE MEMBERS OF THE *SPURS* TEAM JOIN NEXT?

1   *TONY PARKS*

2   *GRAHAM ROBERTS*

3   *PAUL MILLER*

4   *CHRIS HUGHTON*

5   *GARY STEVENS*

6   *STEVE PERRYMAN*

7   *MICKY HAZARD*

8   *TONY GALVIN*

9   *MARK FALCO*

10 *GARTH CROOKS*

11 *RICHARD COOKE*

12 *IAN CULVERHOUSE*

13 *OSVALDO ARDILES*

14 *MARK BOWEN*

15 *ALLY DICK*

TEAM MEMBERS **DANNY THOMAS,** **GARY MABBUTT** AND **RAY CLEMENCE** RETIRED WHEN THEIR **TOTTENHAM** PLAYING DAYS ENDED.

COMING TO AMERICA ...
AND CANADA, TOO!

IN *TOTTENHAM'S* 1960-61 DOUBLE-WINNING SEASON, GOALKEEPER *BILL BROWN* MISSED JUST ONE GAME. THE *SCOTLAND* INTERNATIONAL, A SCOTTISH LEAGUE CUP WINNER WITH *DUNDEE* IN 1952, SPENT SEVEN YEARS AT *WHITE HART LANE*, DURING WHICH TIME HE ADDED ANOTHER FA CUP AND THE EUROPEAN CUP WINNERS' CUP TO HIS MEDAL HAUL. AFTER A SEASON AT *NORTHAMPTON TOWN*, HE SIGNED FOR THE SHORT-LIVED NATIONAL PROFESSIONAL SOCCER LEAGUE SIDE *TORONTO FALCONS* IN 1967. AFTER HIS PLAYING DAYS WERE OVER, *BROWN* STAYED ON IN CANADA, TAKING A POST WITH THE GOVERNMENT. HE DIED IN ONTARIO IN 2014, AGED 73.

1 WHICH FORMER *BLACKBURN ROVERS* AND *SPURS* DEFENDER, WHO MANAGED *WALES* FOR MORE THAN A DECADE, PLAYED FOUR SEASONS WITH THE *SEATTLE SOUNDERS* IN THE LATE 1970S AND INDOOR SOCCER WITH *CLEVELAND FORCE?*

2 NAME ONE OF THE TWO MLS TEAMS FOR WHOM *CLINT DEMPSEY* PLAYED DURING HIS CAREER.

3 WHICH FORMER *TOTTENHAM, LIVERPOOL, ASTON VILLA* AND *BLACKBURN ROVERS* STAR PLAYED FOR *COLUMBUS CREW* IN THE '90S AND MANAGED *NEW ENGLAND REVOLUTION* FROM 2017-19?

4 *ROBBIE KEANE* PLAYED SIX SEASONS WITH WHICH MLS TEAM?

5 *VICTOR WANYAMA* PLAYED IN THE MLS WITH *MONTREAL IMPACT* -- NOW *CF MONTRÉAL* -- WHERE HE WAS MANAGED BY WHICH FORMER *ARSENAL* STAR?

6 WHICH *SOUTH KOREA* STAR, WHOSE PREVIOUS CLUBS INCLUDED *PSV EINDHOVEN, TOTTENHAM HOTSPUR* AND *BORUSSIA DORTMUND,* ENDED HIS CAREER PLAYING IN THE MLS WITH *VANCOUVER WHITECAPS?*

7 DURING HIS TENURE AS MANAGER OF *TORONTO FC* IN 2014, *NEW ZEALAND* INTERNATIONAL *RYAN NELSEN* COACHED WHICH *ENGLAND* STRIKER, HIS FORMER TEAMMATE AT *SPURS?*

8 WHICH *UNITED STATES* INTERNATIONAL DEFENDER JOINED *SPURS* FROM *SEATTLE SOUNDERS* IN 2015, SPENT FIVE SEASONS AT *NEWCASTLE* AND JOINED *GALATASARAY* IN 2021?

9 WHICH *SCOTLAND* DEFENDER, WHO CAPTAINED *SPURS, RANGERS* AND *EVERTON,* PLAYED FOR *KANSAS CITY WIZARDS* AND *SAN JOSE CLASH* IN THE LATE 1990S?

10 WHICH *MILLWALL, SPURS, LEICESTER CITY* AND *FULHAM* GOALKEEPER STARTED HIS SENIOR CAREER WITH THE *PORTLAND TIMBERS* AND ENDED HIS PLAYING DAYS WINNING MULTIPLE HONOURS WITH *SEATTLE SOUNDERS?*

COMINGS AND GOINGS

IN 2021, IN JUST HIS SECOND GAME FOR **ARGENTINA**, CENTRE-BACK DEFENDER **CRISTIAN ROMERO** SCORED HIS FIRST INTERNATIONAL GOAL, HEADING HOME AGAINST **COLOMBIA** AFTER ONLY 130 SECONDS. THE GOAL BROKE THE RECORD FOR THE FASTEST EVER SCORED FOR **ARGENTINA** IN A PROFESSIONAL MATCH, SURPASSING **DIEGO MARADONA'S** GOAL AFTER 168 SECONDS AGAINST **VENEZUELA** IN 1985.

SIGNED ON LOAN FROM **ATALANTA**, **ROMERO** WAS ONE OF THE PLAYERS RECRUITED TO **SPURS** FOLLOWING THE APPOINTMENT OF MANAGER **NUNO ESPÍRITO SANTO** ON JUNE 30, 2021. DURING THE SAME TRANSFER WINDOW, THE FOLLOWING LEFT TO JOIN WHICH CLUBS?

1 JUAN FOYTH

2 TOBY ALDERWEIRELD

3 MOUSSA SISSOKO

4 JOE HART

5 DANNY ROSE

6 PAULO GAZZANIGA

7 ERIK LAMELA

8 PAPE SARR

9 ALFIE WHITEMAN

10 CAMERON CARTER-VICKERS

11 GARETH BALE

12 CARLOS VINÍCIUS

RECORD BREAKERS!

WITH 266 GOALS IN 379 APPEARANCES, *JIMMY GREAVES* SET THE RECORD FOR *TOTTENHAM HOTSPUR* ALL-TIME TOP GOALSCORER.

1 WHOSE £53.8 MILLION TRANSFER FROM *LYON* IN 2019 BROKE THE *TOTTENHAM HOTSPUR* SPENDING RECORD?

2 WHOSE GOAL, AGED 16 YEARS, 163 DAYS, AGAINST *MARINE* IN JANUARY 2021, MADE HIM THE YOUNGEST *SPURS* GOALSCORER?

3 WHO BECAME THE OLDEST FIRST TEAM PLAYER WHEN HE PLAYED AGAINST *NEWCASTLE UNITED* IN 2013 AGED 42 YEARS, 176 DAYS?

4 *TOTTENHAM'S* RECORD WIN WAS A 13-2 FA CUP VICTORY OVER WHICH CLUB IN FEBRUARY OF 1960?

5 WHO MADE A RECORD 854 APPEARANCES FOR *TOTTENHAM HOTSPUR* BETWEEN 1969 AND 1986?

6 THE RECORD ATTENDANCE FOR A *TOTTENHAM* GAME WAS 85,512 AT *WEMBLEY* IN 2016 FOR A UEFA CHAMPIONS LEAGUE FIXTURE AGAINST WHICH TEAM?

7 WHICH PLAYER EARNED A RECORD 74 INTERNATIONAL CAPS DURING HIS TIME AS A *TOTTENHAM* PLAYER?

8 WHO SCORED A RECORD 24 GOALS AS A SUBSTITUTE IN THE PREMIER LEAGUE WITH FIVE DIFFERENT CLUBS?

9 *TOTTENHAM'S* RECORD DEFEAT WAS AN 8-0 THRASHING AT THE HANDS OF WHICH CLUB IN A 1995 INTERTOTO CUP GAME?

10 *TOTTENHAM'S* RECORD PREMIER LEAGUE WIN WAS A 9-1 VICTORY OVER WHICH TEAM IN 2009?

RECORD MAKERS!

IN 1987, *GLENN HODDLE* TEAMED UP WITH HIS *TOTTENHAM* TEAMMATE *CHRIS WADDLE* TO RELEASE TWO POP SINGLES UNDER THE NAME *GLENN AND CHRIS* -- THE FIRST OF WHICH TOOK THE PAIR TO THE NUMBER 12 SPOT ON THE UK CHARTS AND SAW THEM APPEAR ON THE SAME *"TOP OF THE POPS"* SHOW AS *KIM WILDE, JUNIOR, FIVE STAR, TERENCE TRENT D'ARBY* AND *THE SMITHS.* THE DUO'S BUDDING POP CAREER WAS TORPEDOED BY *GLENN'S* MOVE TO *MONACO*

1 WHAT WAS THE TITLE OF THE *GLENN AND CHRIS* SINGLE THAT REACHED NUMBER 12 ON THE POP CHARTS?

2 WRITTEN BY *DAVE PEACOCK* OF *CHAS & DAVE* FAME -- AND PRODUCED BY THE DUO -- WHAT WAS THE TITLE OF THE SONG BY THE *TOTTENHAM HOTSPUR FA CUP FINAL SQUAD* THAT FEATURED *OSSIE ARDILES* AND REACHED NUMBER 5 ON THE POP CHARTS IN 1981?

3 WHAT WAS THE TITLE OF THE "B" SIDE TO THAT 1981 SINGLE, SET TO THE TUNE OF THE AMERICAN CIVIL WAR SONG *"THE BATTLE HYMN OF THE REPUBLIC"?*

4 WHEN *SPURS* REACHED THE FA CUP FINAL AGAIN THE FOLLOWING YEAR, THE SQUAD TEAMED UP WITH *CHAS & DAVE* ONCE MORE FOR WHICH TOP 20 HIT?

5 WHICH *SPURS* AND *SCOTLAND* STAR APPEARED TWICE ON THE SAME EPISODE OF *"TOP OF THE POPS"* IN 1982, FIRSTLY SINGING *"WE HAVE A DREAM"* WITH THE *SCOTLAND WORLD CUP SQUAD STARRING B. A. ROBERTSON* AND THEN ALONGSIDE HIS *SPURS* TEAMMATES AND *CHAS & DAVE* SINGING THAT 1982 HIT?

6 TO CELEBRATE REACHING THE 1987 FA CUP FINAL, THE SQUAD TEAMED UP WITH *CHAS & DAVE* AGAIN ON WHICH TOP 20 HIT?

7 *PAUL GASCOIGNE* TEAMED UP WITH WHICH GROUP TO HIT NUMBER 2 ON THE POP CHARTS IN 1990 WITH HIS VERSION OF THEIR *"FOG ON THE TYNE"* SONG?

8 THE ASSOCIATION WITH *CHAS & DAVE* WAS REVIVED WHEN *TOTTENHAM* REACHED THE 1991 FA CUP FINAL WITH WHICH SINGLE?

9 *CHRIS WADDLE* TEAMED UP WITH WHICH *MARSEILLE* TEAMMATE -- A FRENCH INTERNATIONAL WHO SUBSEQUENTLY WON A LEAGUE TITLE WITH *RANGERS* -- ON THE 1991 SINGLE *"WE'VE GOT A FEELING"?*

THE BOY FROM BECKTON

JERMAIN DEFOE WAS 17 WHEN HE MADE HIS SENIOR DEBUT AND 38 YEARS OLD WHEN HE WON HIS FIRST LEAGUE TITLE. CAPPED 57 TIMES BY *ENGLAND* -- FOR WHOM HE SCORED 20 GOALS -- THE STRIKER HAD TWO SPELLS AT *TOTTENHAM*, AMOUNTING TO A TOTAL OF ELEVEN SEASONS.

AT WHICH CLUBS DID HE PLAY UNDER THE FOLLOWING MANAGERS?

1 EDDIE HOWE

2 TONY ADAMS

3 ANDRÉ VILLAS-BOAS

4 DAVID MOYES

5 RYAN NELSEN

6 DICK ADVOCAAT

7 STEVEN GERRARD

8 GLENN ROEDER

9 SAM ALLARDYCE

10 DAVID PLEAT

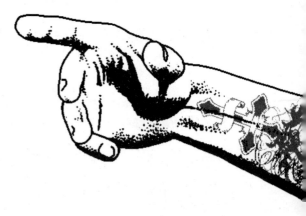

A ROYAL TITLE

EMERSON APARECIDO LEITE DE SOUZA JUNIOR IS BETTER KNOWN AS **EMERSON ROYAL**. HE WAS GIVEN THE NICKNAME AS A YOUNGSTER WHEN AN UNCLE SAID THAT HE RESEMBLED THE MASCOT OF THE **ROYAL** BRAND OF GELATINE DESSERT SOLD IN BRAZIL. HE WON THE TOULON TOURNAMENT WITH THE **BRAZIL U-23** TEAM IN 2019, THE SAME YEAR HE LEFT BRAZIL TO SIGN FOR **BARCELONA**. HE JOINED TOTTENHAM IN A £25.8 MILLION DEAL IN 2021.

HOW ARE THE FOLLOWING **SPURS** PLAYERS BETTER KNOWN?

1   JOSÉ PAULO BEZERRA MACIEL JÚNIOR

2   AHMED HOSSAM HUSSEIN ABDELHAMID

3   MOHAMED ALÍ AMAR

DRAGON'S MEN

GARETH BALE EARNED HIS FIRST CAP IN 2006, BECOMING THE YOUNGEST PLAYER TO REPRESENT **WALES** TO THAT POINT. 12 YEARS LATER, IN 2018, HE SURPASSED THE GOAL TALLY OF **IAN RUSH** TO BECOME HIS COUNTRY'S LEADING ALL-TIME GOALSCORER.

NAME THESE OTHER **WALES** INTERNATIONAL **TOTTENHAM** PLAYERS:

1 A LEAGUE CUP WINNER WITH **SWANSEA CITY** IN 2013, LEFT-BACK WHO JOINED **TOTTENHAM** IN 2014 TAKING THE NUMBER 33 SHIRT.

2 FULL-BACK CAPPED 34 TIMES, HE REPRESENTED **WALES** AT THE 1958 WORLD CUP, WAS A DOUBLE-WINNER WITH **SPURS** IN 1961 AND JOINED **BRIGHTON & HOVE ALBION** IN 1964 AFTER 12 YEARS WITH **TOTTENHAM**.

3 A LEAGUE TITLE WINNER WITH **LEEDS UNITED** IN 1974, HE WAS THE FIRST WELSHMAN TO PLAY IN A EUROPEAN CUP FINAL. HE MOVED ON TO **COVENTRY CITY** BEFORE JOINING **SPURS** IN 1979. CAPPED 59 TIMES BY **WALES**, HE LATER MANAGED THE NATIONAL TEAM.

4 CENTRE-BACK SIGNED FROM **BLACKBURN ROVERS** IN 1966, HE WON THE FA CUP, TWO LEAGUE CUPS AND THE UEFA CUP WITH **TOTTENHAM**. CAPPED 49 TIMES, HE LATER MANAGED **WALES** FROM 1980 UNTIL 1988.

5 HAVING WON PROMOTION WITH **BIRMINGHAM CITY**, HE WON TWO LEAGUE TITLES AND THE UEFA CUP WINNERS' CUP WITH **EVERTON** BEFORE WINNING THE FA CUP IN 1991 WITH **TOTTENHAM**. BORN IN BELGIUM, HIS BRITISH CITIZENSHIP MEANT HE WAS ELIGIBLE TO PLAY FOR ANY OF THE HOME NATIONS AND HE CHOSE **WALES**.

6 CENTRE-BACK SIGNED FROM **SWANSEA CITY** IN 2020, HE WAS ONE OF THREE **SPURS** PLAYERS IN THE **WALES** EURO 2020 SQUAD.

7 CAPPED 41 TIMES, HE PLAYED 399 TIMES FOR **NORWICH CITY** AFTER LEAVING **SPURS** IN 1987. HE WAS ASSISTANT MANAGER TO **MARK HUGHES** AT **BLACKBURN ROVERS**, **MANCHESTER CITY**, **FULHAM**, **QPR**, **STOKE CITY** AND **SOUTHAMPTON**.

8   CAPPED 58 TIMES, HE SPENT FIVE YEARS WITH *SPURS* AFTER LEAVING *PETERBOROUGH UNITED* IN 2000. HE LATER PLAYED FOR *EVERTON* AND *FULHAM*.

9   FIRST WELSHMAN TO EARN 100 CAPS, HE PLAYED FOR *CARDIFF CITY*, *SPURS*, *NOTTINGHAM FOREST* AND *READING* BEFORE JOINING *CHARLTON ATHLETIC* IN 2020.

SPURS CELEBS!

WHEN *JIMMY GREAVES* WAS HOSPITALISED IN 2020, HIS AGENT REVEALED THAT ROCK STAR *PHIL COLLINS* HAD MADE A SUBSTANTIAL FINANCIAL CONTRIBUTION TO HELP FUND CARE FOR THE 80-YEAR-OLD, WHO HAD BEEN WHEELCHAIR-BOUND AND UNABLE TO SPEAK FOLLOWING A STROKE FIVE YEARS EARLIER. *COLLINS* IS A LIFE-LONG *SPURS* FAN WHO HAD IDOLISED *GREAVES* AS A YOUNGSTER.

IDENTIFY THESE OTHER *SPURS*-SUPPORTING CELEBRITIES:

1 OSCAR-NOMINATED ACTOR WHOSE ROLES INCLUDE *DICKIE GREENLEAF, ERROL FLYNN, DR. JOHN WATSON* AND *POPE PIUS XIII*

2 *COUNSELLOR DEANNA TROI* ON THE TV SERIES *"STAR TREK: THE NEXT GENERATION"* AND FOUR *"STAR TREK"* MOVIES

3 AUTHOR OF *"THE SATANIC VERSES"* AND *"MIDNIGHT'S CHILDREN"*, KNIGHTED BY *QUEEN ELIZABETH II* IN 2007.

4 ROCK AND ROLL HALL OF FAMER WHOSE FIVE-PIECE BAND HIT THE CHARTS IN THE 1960S WITH *"GLAD ALL OVER"* AND *"BITS AND PIECES"* AND WHO WROTE THE STAGE MUSICAL *"TIME"*

5 TRINIDADIAN-BRITISH NEWSREADER AND JOURNALIST, *"NEWS AT TEN"* PRESENTER KNIGHTED IN 1999

6 HUGELY SUCCESSFUL AUTHOR, CREATOR OF AN INCREDIBLY POPULAR FANTASY SERIES, WHO ALSO WRITES CRIME FICTION UNDER THE PEN NAME *ROBERT GALBRAITH*

7 OSCAR-NOMINATED, CLASSICALLY TRAINED ACTOR AND DIRECTOR, HIS FILM ROLES INCLUDE *HERCULE POIROT, LAURENCE OLIVIER, GILDEROY LOCKHART, PRINCE HAMLET* AND *IAGO*

8 VETERAN COMEDY ACTOR OF *"CARRY ON", "DOCTOR IN THE HOUSE"* AND *"THE NAVY LARK"* FAME, KNOWN FOR THE CATCHPHRASES *"HELLO"* AND *"DING DONG"*

9 OSCAR, GOLDEN GLOBE AND GRAMMY AWARD-WINNING SINGER, WHOSE CHART-TOPPING HITS INCLUDE *"ROLLING IN THE DEEP"*, *"SOMEONE LIKE YOU"* AND *"SET FIRE TO THE RAIN"*

10 REAL NAME *JOHN WARDLE*, HE WAS BASSIST IN THE BAND *PUBLIC IMAGE LTD* BEFORE FORMING *INVADERS OF THE HEART*

11 THE HIGHEST-GROSSING STAND-UP COMEDIAN IN THE WORLD IN 2012, HE REGULARLY HOSTS SATURDAY EVENING SHOWS ON BBC ONE

12 ACTOR WHOSE ROLES INCLUDED *TRIGGER* ON *"ONLY FOOLS AND HORSES"*, *OWEN NEWITT* ON *"THE VICAR OF DIBLEY"* AND *BARTY CROUCH, SR.* IN *"HARRY POTTER AND THE GOBLET OF FIRE"*

13 AKA *RON WEASLEY*

THE HOD SQUADS

GLENN HODDLE'S FIRST JOB IN MANAGEMENT CAME IN 1991 WHEN HE WAS APPOINTED PLAYER/MANAGER OF STRUGGLING *SWINDON TOWN.* HE STEERED THE CLUB INTO THE PREMIER LEAGUE, BEFORE ACCEPTING THE PLAYER/MANAGER JOB AT *CHELSEA.*

WHICH *SPURS* BOSS ALSO MANAGED THE FOLLOWING TEAMS:

1 *EXETER CITY, BRISTOL ROVERS, QUEENS PARK RANGERS*

2 *NUNEATON BOROUGH, LUTON TOWN, LEICESTER CITY, SHEFFIELD WEDNESDAY*

3 *HULL CITY, NORTHERN IRELAND, ARSENAL*

4 *WORKINGTON, SCUNTHORPE UNITED, BAHRAIN, SPORTING CLUBE DE PORTUGAL, GILLINGHAM, PAHANG, WEST BROMWICH ALBION, ABERDEEN*

5 *AFC BOURNEMOUTH, WEST HAM UNITED, PORTSMOUTH, SOUTHAMPTON, QUEENS PARK RANGERS, JORDAN, BIRMINGHAM CITY*

6 *SHEFFIELD WEDNESDAY, BARNET, GRAYS ATHLETIC*

7 *LISIEUX, TOULOUSE, LILLE, SAINT-ÉTIENNE, SOCHAUX, LYON, FRANCE, AUXERRE*

8 *ESPANYOL, SOUTHAMPTON, PARIS SAINT-GERMAIN*

9 *CRYSTAL PALACE, QUEENS PARK RANGERS, BARCELONA, ENGLAND, AUSTRALIA, MIDDLESBROUGH, LEEDS UNITED*

10 *WIL, GRASSHOPPER, BASEL, VFB STUTTGART, YOUNG BOYS, AL-AHLI, ZAMALEK, SCHALKE 04*

11 *ELCHE LICITANO, ALCOYANO, LEVANTE, LOGROÑÉS, BARCELONA B, LLEIDA, RAYO VALLECANO, BETIS, ESPANYOL, MÁLAGA, SEVILLA, REAL MADRID, CSKA MOSCOW, DNIPRO DNIPROPETROVSK*

SEVILLA SERVICE

WINGER **BRYAN GIL** HAS REPRESENTED **SPAIN** AT EVERY LEVEL FROM U-16 TO THE SENIOR TEAM. HE JOINED **TOTTENHAM** FROM **SEVILLA** IN 2021 FOR A FEE REPORTED TO BE £21.6 MILLION.

IDENTIFY THESE OTHERS WITH CONNECTIONS TO **SEVILLA** AND **SPURS:**

1 CAPPED A RECORD 123 TIMES BY **IVORY COAST**, MIDFIELDER WHO JOINED **SPURS** IN 2006 FROM **SAINT-ÉTIENNE**. A LEAGUE CUP WINNER IN 2008, HE JOINED **SEVILLA** THE FOLLOWING YEAR.

2 FRENCH-BORN **MALI** INTERNATIONAL WHO JOINED **SPURS** FROM **WEST HAM UNITED** IN 2003, HE JOINED **SEVILLA** TWO YEARS LATER. HIS TIME IN SPAIN YIELDED TWO UEFA CUPS, TWO COPA DEL REYS AND EARNED HIM AN AFRICAN FOOTBALLER OF THE YEAR AWARD.

3 **ARGENTINA** INTERNATIONAL FORWARD WHO WAS A COPPA ITALIA RUNNER-UP WITH **ROMA**, A LOSING FINALIST IN TWO LEAGUE CUPS AND THE UEFA CHAMPIONS LEAGUE WITH **SPURS** AND TWICE A RUNNER-UP IN THE COPA AMÉRICA WITH **ARGENTINA**. HE LEFT **TOTTENHAM** FOR **SEVILLA** IN 2021.

4 **ARGENTINA** INTERNATIONAL CENTRE-BACK WHO JOINED **SPURS** FROM **SEVILLA** IN 2014 AND WAS RED-CARDED AGAINST **MANCHESTER CITY** ON HIS DEBUT, AND THEN SENT OFF THREE WEEKS LATER IN THE EUROPA LEAGUE. LOANED BACK TO **SEVILLA** IN EARLY 2016, HE SIGNED FOR **ROMA** IN 2017.

5 **ROMANIA** FORWARD WHO JOINED **SPURS** AFTER THE 1994 WORLD CUP, HE WAS LOANED OUT TO **SEVILLA** IN 1995 AND JOINED **WEST HAM UNITED** THE FOLLOWING YEAR.

THE GHOST OF WHITE HART LANE

HIS PALE COMPLEXION AND ELUSIVE MOVEMENT TO FIND SPACE IN A GAME EARNED **JOHN WHITE** THE NICKNAME **"THE GHOST".** UNTHINKABLE TRAGEDY STRUCK IN 1964 WHEN THE **TOTTENHAM** MIDFIELDER WAS KILLED BY A LIGHTNING STRIKE WHILE SHELTERING UNDER A TREE DURING A THUNDERSTORM ON A LONDON GOLF COURSE. THE **SCOTLAND** INTERNATIONAL WAS ONLY 27 YEARS OLD.

WHITE WAS INDUCTED INTO THE SCOTTISH FOOTBALL HALL OF FAME IN 2005. IDENTIFY THESE OTHER INDUCTEES WITH **SPURS** CONNECTIONS:

1 PLAYED FOR **HEARTS, SPURS, DERBY COUNTY** AND **SWINDON TOWN** AND MANAGED **DERBY** TO A LEAGUE TITLE.

2 LAUNCHED HIS CAREER AT **TOTTENHAM** BEFORE WINNING HONOURS AT **MIDDLESBROUGH, LIVERPOOL, SAMPDORIA** AND **RANGERS** AND MANAGING TEAMS IN ENGLAND, SCOTLAND, TURKEY, ITALY AND PORTUGAL.

3 **TOTTENHAM** GOALKEEPER CAPPED 28 TIMES BY **SCOTLAND** BETWEEN 1958 AND 1965.

4 **CHELSEA, ARSENAL** AND **MANCHESTER UNITED** MIDFIELDER WHO MANAGED **MILLWALL, ARSENAL, LEEDS** AND **SPURS.**

5 STRIKER WHO WON THE 1967 FA CUP, TWO LEAGUE CUPS AND THE 1972 UEFA CUP WITH **SPURS.**

6 STRIKER WHOSE CLUBS INCLUDED **ABERDEEN, SPURS, BARCELONA, BLACKBURN ROVERS** AND **FULHAM.**

7 CAPTAINED **SPURS** IN THE 1987 FA CUP FINAL BEFORE CAPTAINING **RANGERS** TO NINE SUCCESSIVE SCOTTISH LEAGUE TITLES.

8 LEGENDARY **LEEDS UNITED, MANCHESTER UNITED** AND **AC MILAN** STRIKER WHO WAS AN ASSISTANT TO **HARRY REDKNAPP** AT **PORTSMOUTH, SPURS** AND **QUEENS PARK RANGERS.**

THE GOALS THAT BROUGHT THE GLORY!

FA CUP HOLDERS *TOTTENHAM* RETURNED TO WEMBLEY IN 1982 TO DEFEND THEIR CROWN AGAINST *QUEENS PARK RANGERS*, WHO WERE MANAGED BY FORMER *SPURS* STAR -- AND FUTURE *TOTTENHAM* MANAGER -- *TERRY VENABLES*. THE GAME WENT INTO EXTRA-TIME, DURING WHICH *GLENN HODDLE'S* 110TH MINUTE OPENER WAS CANCELLED OUT BY *TERRY FENWICK'S* EQUALISER. THE TWO TEAMS MET AGAIN FIVE DAYS LATER, *HODDLE'S* EARLY PENALTY GOAL PROVING ENOUGH TO GIVE *SPURS* VICTORY.

WHO SCORED FOR *TOTTENHAM* IN THE FOLLOWING FA CUP FINALS?

1   1901 V *SHEFFIELD UNITED* -- DREW 2-2

2   1901 REPLAY V *SHEFFIELD UNITED* -- WON 3-1

3   1921 V *WOLVERHAMPTON WANDERERS* -- WON 1-0

4   1961 V *LEICESTER CITY* -- WON 2-0

5   1962 V *BURNLEY* -- WON 3-1

6   1967 V *CHELSEA* -- WON 2-1

7   1981 V *MANCHESTER CITY* -- DREW 1-1

8   1981 REPLAY V *MANCHESTER CITY* -- WON 3-2

9   1987 V *COVENTRY CITY* -- LOST 3-2

10   1991 V *NOTTINGHAM FOREST* -- WON 2-1

SHOW ME THE MONEY!

HAVING WON THE 2008 LEAGUE CUP WITH **SPURS**, **DIMITAR BERBATOV** JOINED **MANCHESTER UNITED** IN 2008 IN A £30.75 MILLION DEAL. IT WAS THE HIGHEST TRANSFER FEE THE CLUB HAD EVER RECEIVED TO THAT POINT AND WOULD REMAIN SO UNTIL THE SALE OF **LUKA MODRIĆ**.

IDENTIFY THESE PLAYERS SOLD BY **TOTTENHAM**:

1 £53 MILLION: *MANCHESTER CITY*, 2017

2 £18.6 MILLION: *MANCHESTER UNITED*, 2006

3 £18 MILLION: *STOKE CITY*, 2017

4 £19 MILLION: *LIVERPOOL*, 2008

5 £17 MILLION: *SCHALKE 04*, 2017

6 £86.3 MILLION: *REAL MADRID*, 2013

7 £20 MILLION: *ATLÉTICO MADRID*, 2019

8 £18 MILLION: *INTERNAZIONALE*, 2020

"SECOND IS NOTHING"

IN 1962-63, A SEASON IN WHICH *TOTTENHAM* FINISHED RUNNERS-UP IN THE LEAGUE, *JIMMY GREAVES* -- WITH 37 GOALS -- WAS THE TOP GOALSCORER IN THE TOP FLIGHT.

IT WAS *JOSÉ MOURINHO* WHO DECLARED THAT *"SECOND IS NOTHING"* ... BUT CAN YOU NAME THE TEAMS TO WHICH *SPURS* FINISHED SECOND IN THESE COMPETITIONS?

1 1922: FIRST DIVISION, LOST BY 6PTS

2 1952: FIRST DIVISION, LOST BY 4PTS

3 1957: FIRST DIVISION, LOST BY 8PTS

4 1963: FIRST DIVISION, LOST BY 6PTS

5 1974: UEFA CUP, LOST 4-2 ON AGGREGATE

6 1982: LEAGUE CUP, LOST 3-1

7 1987: FA CUP, LOST 3-2

8 2002: LEAGUE CUP, LOST 2-1

9 2009: LEAGUE CUP, LOST ON PENALTIES

10 2015: LEAGUE CUP, LOST 2-0

11 2017: PREMIER LEAGUE, LOST BY 7PTS

12 2019: UEFA CHAMPIONS LEAGUE, LOST 2-0

13 2021: LEAGUE CUP, LOST 1-0

NOT THE FACE!
NOT THE FACE!

HAVING LEFT **SPURS** FOR **LAZIO**, **PAUL GASCOIGNE** WAS ON THE RECEIVING END OF A **JAN WOUTERS** ELBOW PLAYING FOR **ENGLAND** AGAINST THE **NETHERLANDS** IN A 1994 WORLD CUP QUALIFIER, THE BROKEN CHEEKBONE HE RECEIVED NECESSITATED **GAZZA** WEARING A PROTECTIVE FACE MASK FOR THE REST OF THE SEASON.

NAME THESE OTHER **SPURS** PLAYERS WHO RECEIVED FACIAL INJURIES:

1 HAVING SUSTAINED A FRACTURED SKULL AND EYE SOCKET COURTESY OF **JOHN FASHANU'S** ELBOW IN A GAME AGAINST **WIMBLEDON** IN 1993, WHO BECAME THE FIRST PLAYER TO WEAR A PROTECTIVE MASK ON THE FIELD WHEN HE FINALLY RETURNED TO ACTION?

2 WHICH DEFENDER SUFFERED A BROKEN NOSE AGAINST **BOCA JUNIORS** IN THE PEACE CUP TOURNAMENT IN SUMMER, 2005?

3 WEEKS AFTER SIGNING FROM **RED STAR BELGRADE** IN 2001, WHICH SERBIAN DEFENDER SUFFERED A BROKEN CHEEKBONE IN A GAME AGAINST **CHELSEA**, RESULTING IN HIM PLAYING JUST TWO MORE GAMES IN HIS DEBUT SEASON?

4 NAME THE ROMANIAN WHO, HAVING BROKEN HIS NOSE IN A GAME AGAINST **NEWCASTLE** IN 2013, SCORED THE ONLY LEAGUE GOAL OF HIS **SPURS** CAREER WHILE WEARING A FACEMASK AGAINST **FULHAM?**

5 NAME THE FULL-BACK WHOSE NOSE AND UPPER JAW WERE SMASHED IN A COLLISION WITH **LIVERPOOL'S IAN ST JOHN** IN 1959, INJURIES SO SEVERE HE WAS OUT OF ACTION FOR TWO YEARS.

6 WHO LOST THREE TEETH IN THE 1981 FA CUP FINAL?

7 IN 2016, HAVING BROKEN HIS NOSE A MONTH EARLIER, WHO SCORED A GOAL AGAINST **ARSENAL** AND RIPPED OFF HIS PROTECTIVE MASK IN CELEBRATION?

8 A HEAD INJURY SUSTAINED IN A COLLISION WITH TEAMMATE *TOBY ALDERWEIRELD* IN A 2019 GAME AGAINST *AJAX* RESULTED IN WHICH DEFENDER HAVING TO WEAR A PROTECTIVE MASK IN SUBSEQUENT GAMES, LATER REVEALING HE SUFFERED HEADACHES AND DIZZINESS FOR NINE MONTHS AFTER THE INCIDENT?

9 WHICH GOALKEEPER'S JAW WAS FRACTURED IN A COLLISION WITH *MANCHESTER UNITED'S JOE JORDAN* IN A 1980 FA CUP GAME, RESULTING IN *GLENN HODDLE* HAVING TO GO IN GOAL FOR THE REST OF THE MATCH?

10 IN 2016, WHICH *ENGLAND* INTERNATIONAL DEFENDER PLAYED GAMES AGAINST *ARSENAL*, *WEST HAM UNITED* AND *MONACO* WEARING A BLACK PROTECTIVE FACEMASK?

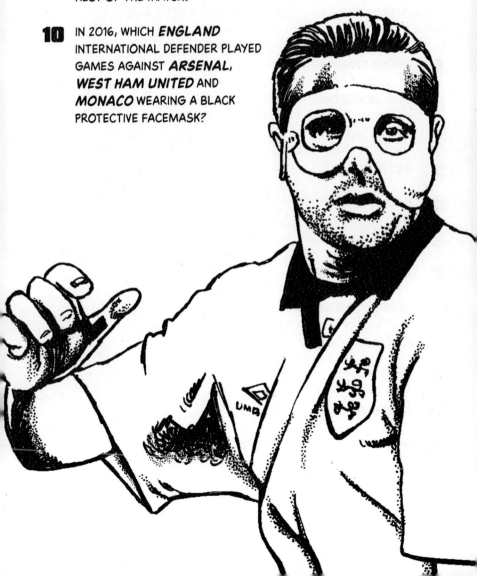

"DILLINGER"

ONE OF THE FIRST **TOTTENHAM** PLAYERS TO OWN A CAR, HIS CHOICE OF VEHICLE -- A LARGE AMERICAN CADILLAC -- EARNED **TED DITCHBURN** THE NICKNAME OF **"DILLINGER"**, AFTER THE INFAMOUS GANGSTER. HE PLAYED 452 TIMES FOR **SPURS**, INCLUDING A RUN OF 247 CONSECUTIVE LEAGUE APPEARANCES. A KEY FIGURE IN THE TEAM THAT WON A BACK-TO-BACK PROMOTION AND TOP FLIGHT TITLE, **DITCHBURN'S TOTTENHAM** CAREER WAS DERAILED BY A BROKEN FINGER AND IN 1959 HE LEFT **SPURS** FOR **ROMFORD** AFTER 20 YEARS AT **WHITE HART LANE**.

DITCHBURN WAS CAPPED SIX TIMES BY **ENGLAND** -- WHICH COUNTRIES DID THESE **TOTTENHAM** GOALKEEPERS REPRESENT?

1   *PAULO GAZZANIGA*

2   *MICHEL VORM*

3   *BILL BROWN*

4   *RADEK ČERNÝ*

5   *ESPEN BAARDSEN*

6   *ERIK THORSTVEDT*

7   *HEURELHO GOMES*

8   *LARS HIRSCHFELD*

9   *PAU LÓPEZ*

10 *FRODE GRODÅS*

THE BOYS OF '72

PLAYED OVER TWO LEGS, THE 1972 UEFA CUP FINAL WAS THE FIRST UEFA CLUB COMPETITION FINAL PLAYED BETWEEN CLUBS FROM THE SAME ASSOCIATION. *MARTIN CHIVERS* SCORED A BRACE IN THE FIRST LEG TO GIVE *SPURS* A 2-1 ADVANTAGE OVER *WOLVERHAMPTON WANDERERS* AND A 1-1 DRAW IN THE RETURN GAME SECURED VICTORY.

WHICH CLUBS DID THE MEMBERS OF THAT 1972 TEAM SIGN FOR AFTER
LEAVING *SPURS?*

1 *PAT JENNINGS*

2 *JOE KINNEAR*

3 *ALAN MULLERY*

4 *MIKE ENGLAND*

5 *PHIL BEAL*

6 *ALAN GILZEAN*

7 *STEVE PERRYMAN*

8 *MARTIN CHIVERS*

9 *MARTIN PETERS*

10 *RALPH COATES*

11 *RAY EVANS*

12 *BARRY DAINES*

13 *TERRY NAYLOR*

14 *JOHN PRATT*

TEAM MEMBERS *CYRIL KNOWLES* AND *JIMMY PEARCE* RETIRED
AFTER PLAYING FOR *SPURS.*

"EL TEL"

AS A PLAYER, **TERRY VENABLES** WON HONOURS WITH **CHELSEA** AND **SPURS**, HELPED **QUEENS PARK RANGERS** GAIN PROMOTION TO THE TOP FLIGHT AND ENDED HS PLAYING DAYS AT **CRYSTAL PALACE**. HE THEN EMBARKED ON THE MANAGEMENT CAREER THAT SAW HIM WIN HONOURS WITH **CRYSTAL PALACE**, **QPR** AND **SPURS**, MANAGE **ENGLAND** AND STEER **BARCELONA** TO A FIRST LEAGUE TITLE IN 11 YEARS. DURING HIS TIME IN SPAIN, THE ENGLISH PRESS DUBBED HIM **"EL TEL"**.

IDENTIFY THESE **SPURS** PLAYERS WHO PLAYED FOR **BARCELONA**:

1 CAPPED 115 TIMES BY **ROMANIA**, HE WON LEAGUE TITLES WITH **STEAUA BUCUREȘTI** AND **PSV EINDHOVEN**, AND THREE LEAGUE TITLES AND THE UEFA CUP WITH **GALATASARAY**. HE LEFT **SPURS** AFTER ONE SEASON TO JOIN **BARCELONA** IN 1995, WITH WHOM HE WON THE UEFA CUP WINNERS' CUP.

2 CAPPED 107 TIMES BY **MEXICO**, HE GRADUATED FROM **BARCELONA'S LA MASIA** ACADEMY AND JOINED **SPURS** IN 2008, WHERE HE SPENT MUCH OF HIS FOUR SEASONS WITH THE CLUB ON LOAN AT **IPSWICH TOWN**, **RACING SANTANDER** AND **GALATASARAY**. HE LATER PLAYED FOR **LA GALAXY** BEFORE RETURNING TO MEXICO TO JOIN **AMÉRICA** IN 2019.

3 MIDFIELDER WHO BEGAN HIS CAREER AT **BARCELONA**, THEN WON THE 1991 FA CUP WITH **TOTTENHAM**, BEFORE JOINING **REAL ZARAGOZA** -- WHERE HE FURTHER ENDEARED HIMSELF TO **SPURS** FANS WHEN HE LOBBED **ARSENAL'S DAVID SEAMAN** FROM 40 YARDS TO SCORE THE LAST-MINUTE GOAL THAT WON THE 1995 UEFA CUP WINNERS' CUP FINAL!

4 CAPPED 74 TIMES BY THE **NETHERLANDS**, HE WON THREE LEAGUE TITLES, THE CHAMPIONS LEAGUE AND THE UEFA CUP WITH **AJAX**, BEFORE EMBARKING ON A CAREER THAT TOOK HIM TO BOTH **MILAN** CLUBS, **JUVENTUS**, **SPURS**, **BARCELONA** AND MORE!

5 **BRAZIL** INTERNATIONAL RIGHT-BACK WHO JOINED **SPURS** FROM **BARCELONA** FOR £25.8 MILLION IN THE SUMMER OF 2021.

6 CAPPED 88 TIMES BY *ICELAND*, HE PLAYED IN ENGLAND WITH *BOLTON WANDERERS*, *CHELSEA*, *SPURS* AND *STOKE CITY* AND WON THE CHAMPIONS LEAGUE IN 2009 WITH *BARCELONA*.

7 GERMAN-BORN *GHANA* INTERNATIONAL, HE SPENT THREE SEASONS WITH *SPURS*, WON LA LIGA IN 2019 WITH *BARCELONA*, AND PLAYED IN GERMANY, ITALY AND TURKEY.

8 STRIKER WHO PLAYED FOR *LEICESTER CITY*, *EVERTON*, *BARCELONA*, *TOTTENHAM* AND *NAGOYA GRAMPUS*.

THE BOYS OF '63

WITH THE 5-1 THRASHING OF *ATLÉTICO MADRID* IN THE EUROPEAN CUP WINNERS' CUP FINAL IN ROTTERDAM IN 1963, *TOTTENHAM HOTSPUR* BECAME THE FIRST ENGLISH CLUB TO WIN A MAJOR EUROPEAN COMPETITION. *TERRY DYSON* AND *JIMMY GREAVES* -- PICTURED HERE WITH THE TROPHY -- GRABBED TWO GOALS APIECE, WITH A GOAL FROM *JOHN WHITE* COMPLETING THE ROUT.

LEFT-BACK *RON HENRY* CAME THROUGH THE RANKS AT *SPURS* -- BUT FROM WHICH CLUBS WERE THE OTHER MEMBERS OF THAT WINNING TEAM RECRUITED?

1 BILL BROWN

2 PETER BAKER

3 MAURICE NORMAN

4 DANNY BLANCHFLOWER

5 TONY MARCHI

6 JOHN WHITE

7 CLIFF JONES

8 JIMMY GREAVES

9 BOBBY SMITH

10 TERRY DYSON

THE HONDURAN

CAPPED 97 TIMES BY **HONDURAS**, **WILSON PALACIOS** SPENT THREE SEASONS WITH **TOTTENHAM** BETWEEN 2009 AND 2011. IN 2009, IN THE EARLY HOURS OF THE MORNING AT A HOTEL IN LIVERPOOL WHERE **SPURS** WERE STAYING BEFORE A GAME AT **EVERTON**, HE RECEIVED A PHONE CALL FROM HIS MOTHER INFORMING HIM THAT HIS 16-YEAR-OLD BROTHER HAD BEEN MURDERED BY KIDNAPPERS. NOT WISHING TO DISRUPT THE TEAM'S PREPARATIONS, **PALACIOS** PACKED HIS BAGS AND SAT QUIETLY IN THE HOTEL LOBBY WAITING FOR MANAGER **HARRY REDKNAPP** TO SURFACE THE NEXT MORNING SO HE COULD ASK PERMISSION TO FLY HOME TO BE WITH HIS GRIEVING FAMILY. THE FOLLOWING YEAR, WILSON WAS A MEMBER OF THE HONDURAS WORLD CUP SQUAD, ALONG WITH HIS BROTHERS **JERRY** AND **JOHNNY** -- THE FIRST TRIO OF BROTHERS TO REPRESENT A SINGLE NATION IN THE WORLD CUP.

1 **PALACIOS** GOT HIS FIRST TASTE OF ENGLISH FOOTBALL IN 2007, PLAYING ON LOAN AT WHICH CLUB UNDER **STEVE BRUCE?**

2 HE FOLLOWED **BRUCE** TO WHICH CLUB IN EARLY 2008?

3 **HARRY REDKNAPP** TOOK **PALACIOS** TO **SPURS** IN A £12 MILLION DEAL IN EARLY 2009. IN 2011, HE WAS TRANSFERRED TO **STOKE CITY** ON THE SAME DAY AS WHICH **TOTTENHAM** TEAMMATE?

4 HE SIGNED FOR WHICH MAJOR LEAGUE SOCCER TEAM IN 2016?

oma

POACHERS TURNED GAMEKEEPERS

AFTER LAUNCHING HIS CAREER WITH **SOUTHEND UNITED**, **PETER TAYLOR** WAS PLAYING IN THE THIRD TIER OF LEAGUE FOOTBALL WITH **CRYSTAL PALACE** WHEN HE WON THE FIRST OF HIS FOUR **ENGLAND** CAPS IN 1976, HE WENT ON TO PLAY FOR A NUMBER OF CLUBS, INCLUDING SPURS, BEFORE GOING INTO MANAGEMENT, HE TOOK THE REINS WITH A SCORE OF TEAMS -- INCLUDING FORMER CLUBS **SOUTHEND UNITED** AND **CRYSTAL PALACE**.

A NUMBER OF PLAYERS OR MANAGERS ASSOCIATED WITH **TOTTENHAM HOTSPUR** MANAGED TEAMS THEY HAD PREVIOUSLY PLAYED FOR, WHO BOTH PLAYED FOR AND MANAGED THE FOLLOWING?

1 MANAGED **TOTTENHAM** 1974-76, PLAYED FOR AND MANAGED **ARSENAL** AND **HULL CITY**.

2 MANAGED **TOTTENHAM** FOUR TIMES INCLUDING IN A CARETAKER ROLE, PLAYED FOR AND MANAGED **LUTON TOWN** TWICE.

3 MANAGED **TOTTENHAM** IN 2004, HAVING PLAYED FOR AND MANAGED **SAINT-ÉTIENNE**.

4 MANAGED **TOTTENHAM** 2014 TO 2019, PLAYED FOR AND MANAGED BOTH **ESPANYOL** AND **PARIS SAINT-GERMAIN**.

5 PLAYED FOR **QUEENS PARK RANGERS** TWICE BEFORE MANAGING THEM TWICE, PLAYED FOR AND MANAGED **EXETER CITY**, PLAYED FOR **BRISTOL ROVERS** AS WELL AS MANAGING THEM TWICE.

6 **SPURS** MANAGER BETWEEN 1976 AND 1984, HE PLAYED FOR AND MANAGED BOTH **WORKINGTON** AND **SCUNTHORPE UNITED**.

THREEPEATS!

IN HIS FIRST TRANSFER WINDOW SINCE BEING APPOINTED MANAGER OF **TOTTENHAM, HARRY REDKNAPP** BROUGHT BACK THREE PLAYERS WHO HAD PREVIOUSLY PLAYED FOR **SPURS** -- **ROBBIE KEANE, JERMAIN DEFOE** AND **PASCAL CHIMBONDA.** THE SIGNING OF **KEANE** INSPIRED **VIRGIN TRAINS** TO RUN AN ADVERTISEMENT WITH THE SLOGAN *"A LIVERPOOL TO LONDON RETURN FASTER THAN ROBBIE KEANE".*

FROM WHICH CLUBS WERE THESE PLAYERS SIGNED DURING **HARRY REDKNAPP'S** FOUR SEASONS AS **TOTTENHAM** BOSS?

1 *JERMAIN DEFOE*

2 *WILSON PALACIOS*

3 *PETER CROUCH*

4 *RAFAEL VAN DER VAART*

5 *SANDRO*

6 *SÉBASTIEN BASSONG*

7 *KYLE NAUGHTON*

8 *KYLE WALKER*

9 *YOUNÈS KABOUL*

10 *SCOTT PARKER*

11 *STEVEN PIENAAR*

12 *PASCAL CHIMBONDA*

13 *NIKO KRANJCAR*

14 *EMMANUEL ADEBAYOR*

15 *IAGO FALQUE*

MR. TOTTENHAM HOTSPUR

DURING HIS 36-YEAR ASSOCIATION WITH THE CLUB, **BILL NICHOLSON** CARVED HIS NAME INTO **TOTTENHAM HOTSPUR** LEGEND. HAVING JOINED THE CLUB AS A TEENAGER, HIS PLAYING DAYS WERE INTERRUPTED BY THE SECOND WORLD WAR, AFTER WHICH HE HELPED THE CLUB WIN PROMOTION IN 1950 AND THE FIRST DIVISION TITLE THE FOLLOWING SEASON. AFTER HANGING UP HIS BOOTS, HE TOOK UP A COACHING ROLE WITH THE CLUB AND ROSE THROUGH THE RANKS TO BECOME MANAGER IN 1958. IN HIS FIRST GAME IN CHARGE, **SPURS** THRASHED **EVERTON** 10-4. HE WENT ON TO WIN EIGHT MAJOR TROPHIES IN HIS 16-YEAR SPELL AT THE HELM, INCLUDING THE LEAGUE AND FA CUP DOUBLE IN 1961 AS WELL AS THE UEFA CUP AND THE EUROPEAN CUP WINNERS' CUP.

NICHOLSON WON THE FA CUP IN 1961, 1962 AND 1967, AND THE LEAGUE CUP IN 1971 AND 1973. WHO MANAGED **SPURS** IN THE FOLLOWING FINALS?

1 1901 FA CUP: **SHEFFIELD UNITED** DREW 2-2, WON REPLAY 3-1

2 1921 FA CUP: **WOLVERHAMPTON WANDERERS** WON 1-0

3 1981 FA CUP: **MANCHESTER CITY** DREW 1-1, WON REPLAY 3-2

4 1982 LEAGUE CUP: **LIVERPOOL** LOST 3-1

5 1982 FA CUP: **QUEENS PARK RANGERS** DREW 1-1, WON REPLAY 1-0

6 1987 FA CUP: **COVENTRY CITY** LOST 3-2

7 1991 FA CUP: **NOTTINGHAM FOREST** WON 2-1

8 1999 LEAGUE CUP: **LEICESTER CITY** WON 1-0

9 2002 LEAGUE CUP: **BLACKBURN ROVERS** LOST 2-1

10 2008 LEAGUE CUP: **CHELSEA** WON 2-1

11 2009 LEAGUE CUP: **MANCHESTER UNITED** LOST ON PENALTIES

12 2015 LEAGUE CUP: **CHELSEA** LOST 2-0

13 2021 LEAGUE CUP: **MANCHESTER CITY** LOST 1-0

HOT SHOTS!

HARRY KANE HAS DOMINATED THE SCORING CHARTS IN RECENT YEARS, NOT ONLY FOR *TOTTENHAM* BUT ALSO WINNING THE PREMIER LEAGUE GOLDEN BOOT A NUMBER OF TIMES. PRIOR TO *KANE'S* EMERGENCE AS A TOP CLASS STRIKER, *EMMANUEL ADEBAYOR* TOPPED THE TOTTENHAM GOALSCORING LIST IN TWO OF HIS FOUR SEASONS AT THE CLUB.

IDENTIFY THESE OTHER PLAYERS WHO WERE *TOTTENHAM'S* TOP GOALSCORER IN PREVIOUS SEASONS:

1 STRIKER CAPPED 79 TIMES BY *NORWAY*, A LEAGUE CUP WINNER WITH *SPURS* IN 1999, HE WAS THE CLUB'S TOP SCORER 1N 1998-99 WITH 13 GOALS AND 1999-2000 WITH 17 GOALS.

2 HE SCORED 26 GOALS IN THE 2012-13 SEASON BEFORE HIS WORLD RECORD MOVE TO SPANISH FOOTBALL.

3 FORMER *DUNDEE* FORWARD WHO JOINED *SPURS* IN 1975, HE WAS THE CLUB'S TOP SCORER IN THREE OF HIS FOUR FULL SEASONS AT *WHITE HART LANE*, SCORING 12 GOALS IN 1975-76, 25 GOALS THE FOLLOWING SEASON AND 20 GOALS IN 1977-78, BEFORE MOVING ON TO *DERBY COUNTY* IN SEPTEMBER, 1978.

4 FORWARD WHO TOPPED THE GOALSCORING CHARTS SIX OF THE SEVEN SEASONS BETWEEN 1955 AND 1961, INCLUDING 1957-58 WHEN HE HIT 38 GOALS, INCLUDING 36 IN THE LEAGUE.

5 URUGUAYAN SIGNED FROM *CHELSEA*, HE SCORED 14 GOALS IN THE 2001-02 SEASON. HE WAS LATER ASSISTANT BOSS AT *TOTTENHAM* EARLY IN HIS EXTENSIVE MANAGEMENT CAREER.

6 *ENGLAND* STRIKER WHO PLAYED FOR *IPSWICH TOWN* AND *CHARLTON ATHLETIC* BEFORE JOINING *SPURS* IN A CLUB-RECORD £16.5 MILLION DEAL IN 2007. HE WAS TOP SCORER WITH 17 GOALS IN HIS SECOND SEASON BEFORE MOVING ON TO *SUNDERLAND*.

7 HIS 49 GOALS -- INCLUDING 33 IN THE LEAGUE -- PROPELLED HIM TO PFA AND FWA PLAYER OF THE YEAR AWARDS IN 1986-87.

PARTY LIKE IT'S 1999

AFTER WINNING HONOURS IN HIS NATIVE FRANCE WITH **PARIS SAINT-GERMAIN**, **DAVID GINOLA** PLAYED FOR FOUR CLUBS IN ENGLAND -- **NEWCASTLE UNITED**, **SPURS**, **ASTON VILLA** AND **EVERTON**. HIS ONLY TROPHY IN EIGHT SEASONS IN ENGLAND WAS THE 1999 LEAGUE CUP.

WHICH CLUBS DID THE FOLLOWING MEMBERS OF **TOTTENHAM'S** VICTORIOUS 1999 TEAM SIGN FOR NEXT?

1 *IAN WALKER*

2 *STEPHEN CARR*

3 *SOL CAMPBELL*

4 *RAMON VEGA*

5 *JUSTIN EDINBURGH*

6 *DARREN ANDERTON*

7 *STEFFEN FREUND*

8 *ALLAN NIELSEN*

9 *LES FERDINAND*

10 *STEFFEN IVERSEN*

11 *ESPEN BAARDSEN*

12 *LUKE YOUNG*

13 *JOSÉ DOMINGUEZ*

14 *ANDY SINTON*

15 *CHRIS ARMSTRONG*

WELL, I NEVER ...

IN HIS *MILLWALL* DAYS, *PAT VAN DEN HAUWE* AND HIS TEAMMATES WOULD PLAY A GAME WHERE THEY PLACED THEIR HAND ON A DARTBOARD AND THE OTHERS WOULD THROW DARTS TO SEE IF THEY COULD MISS THEIR OUTSTRETCHED FINGERS. THEY INVARIABLY COULDN'T.

1 THE LATE 1970S TV SERIES *"HAZELL"*, STARRING *NICHOLAS BALL* AS A WISECRACKING PRIVATE DETECTIVE, WAS BASED ON A SERIES OF BOOKS CO-WRITTEN BY WHICH FORMER *SPURS* PLAYER?

2 WHICH *SPURS* PLAYER HAD APPEARED, WHEN HE WAS 13, IN A TV AD FOR 1994 WORLD CUP SPONSORS *MCDONALD'S* DEMONSTRATING HIS KEEPY-UPPY SKILLS?

3 THE BROTHER OF WHICH *SPURS* AND *ENGLAND* FULL-BACK SENSATIONALLY ABANDONED HIS CAREER AT THE AGE OF 23, DESERTING *WOLVERHAMPTON WANDERERS* IN 1969 TO BECOME A JEHOVAH'S WITNESS?

4 WHICH *TOTTENHAM* PLAYER AND SUBSEQUENT MANAGER SCORED FOR *ENGLAND* WITH HIS FIRST TOUCH IN INTERNATIONAL FOOTBALL -- AND NEVER PLAYED FOR *ENGLAND* AGAIN?

5 IN WHICH 1981 MOVIE DID *OSSIE ARDILES* APPEAR WITH *MICHAEL CAINE* AND *SYLVESTER STALLONE?*

6 WHICH *SPURS* PLAYER WAS MARRIED TO *MANDY SMITH*, WHO HAD PREVIOUSLY MARRIED *BILL WYMAN* OF THE *ROLLING STONES* WHEN SHE WAS 18 AND THE BASS PLAYER WAS 52?

7 WHICH *SPURS* PLAYER DABBLED IN ACTING AFTER RETIRING FROM FOOTBALL, HIS CREDITS INCLUDING *"THE LAST DROP"* -- IN A CAST THAT INCLUDED *BILLY ZANE, RAFE SPALL* AND *ALEXANDER SKARSGÅRD* -- AND TV SOAP *"THE YOUNG AND THE RESTLESS"?*

THE CREATIVE CROATIAN

SIGNED FROM *DINAMO ZAGREB* IN 2008 FOR £16.5 MILLION, *LUKA MODRIĆ* LED *SPURS* TO THEIR FIRST UEFA CHAMPIONS LEAGUE CAMPAIGN IN ALMOST 50 YEARS, THE TEAM REACHING THE QUARTER-FINALS OF THE 2010-11 TOURNAMENT. HE JOINED *REAL MADRID* IN 2012, GOING ON TO WIN A MULTITUDE OF HONOURS IN SPAIN, INCLUDING FOUR UEFA CHAMPIONS LEAGUES, THREE CLUB WORLD CUPS AND TWO LEAGUE TITLES. INDIVIDUAL ACCOLADES INCLUDE THE BALLON D'OR, A WORLD CUP GOLDEN BALL AND THE 2019 GOLDEN FOOT. IN 2020 HE WON THE CROATIAN FOOTBALLER OF THE YEAR AWARD FOR THE NINTH TIME.

1 MODRIĆ MADE HIS DEBUT FOR *CROATIA* IN MARCH, 2006. THE FATHER OF WHICH PLAYER -- WHO WOULD LATER PLAY ALONGSIDE *MODRIĆ* IN THE *TOTTENHAM* TEAM -- GAVE HIM HIS FIRST CAP?

2 WHO WAS THE MANAGER WHO SIGNED *MODRIĆ* TO *SPURS?*

3 *MODRIĆ* PLAYED UNDER WHICH SUBSEQUENT *TOTTENHAM HOTSPUR* MANAGER AT *REAL MADRID?*

4 UNDER WHICH FORMER *WEST HAM UNITED* DEFENDER AND SUBSEQUENT MANAGER DID *LUKA MODRIĆ* PLAY FOR THE *CROATIA* NATIONAL TEAM?

5 *MODRIĆ* WAS ON THE LOSING SIDE IN THE 2018 WORLD CUP FINAL. CAN YOU NAME THE OTHER *TOTTENHAM* PLAYER, PAST OR PRESENT, WHO FEATURED IN THAT GAME?

HAT-TRICK HEROES

SIGNED FROM **CHELSEA** FOR £18,000 IN 1955, **BOBBY SMITH** WAS A BURLY BULLDOZER CENTRE-FORWARD, EXCEPTIONALLY GOOD IN THE AIR FOR A MAN WHO STOOD ONLY 5' 9" TALL. IN THE 1957-58 SEASON HE SCORED 36 LEAGUE GOALS, EQUALLING THE CLUB RECORD SET BY **TED HARPER** 27 YEARS EARLIER. HE HIT 33 GOALS IN THE DOUBLE-WINNING SEASON OF 1960-61, AND SCORED IN TWO FA CUP FINAL WINS. A YEAR AFTER HELPING **SPURS** WIN THE 1963 UEFA CUP WINNERS' CUP, HAVING FALLEN OUT OF FAVOUR, THE YORKSHIREMAN WAS SOLD TO FOURTH-TIER **BRIGHTON & HOVE ALBION**.

BOBBY SMITH SCORED 12 HAT-TRICKS FOR **SPURS**, A TALLY SO FAR BETTERED ONLY BY **JIMMY GREAVES** AND **HARRY KANE**. IDENTIFY THESE **TOTTENHAM** HAT-TRICK HEROES:

1 WHO HIT FIVE GOALS IN A 9-1 **TOTTENHAM** DEMOLITION OF **WIGAN ATHLETIC** IN 2009?

2 WHICH **TOTTENHAM** PLAYER SCORED FIVE GOALS FOR **ENGLAND** AGAINST **NORTHERN IRELAND** IN 1938, INCLUDING THREE IN LESS THAN FOUR MINUTES, THE FASTEST HAT-TRICK IN INTERNATIONAL FOOTBALL!

3 WHO SCORED FIVE GOALS FOR **SPURS** IN A 7-1 LEAGUE WIN OVER **BIRMINGHAM CITY** IN 1957?

4 WHICH TEAM WAS ON THE WRONG END OF AN FA CUP REPLAY 13-2 TRASHING IN 1960, IN WHICH **LES ALLEN** SCORED FIVE, **BOBBY SMITH** GOT FOUR AND **CLIFF JONES** HIT A HAT-TRICK?

5 WHOSE HAT-TRICK IN A MIRACULOUS SECOND-HALF COMEBACK AGAINST **AJAX** IN THE SEMI-FINAL TOOK **SPURS** TO THE 2019 UEFA CHAMPIONS LEAGUE FINAL?

6 **TOTTENHAM'S** 5-2 WIN AT **SOUTHAMPTON** IN 2020 WAS THE FIRST TIME IN PREMIER LEAGUE HISTORY THAT ONE PLAYER SCORED FOUR GOALS ALL LAID ON BY THE SAME TEAMMATE -- WHO WAS THE GOALSCORER AND WHO MADE THOSE ASSISTS?

THE CHRISTIAN WAY

HAVING DISTINGUISHED HIMSELF AT THE DELIGHTFULLY-NAMED *MIDDELFART G&BK*, DANISH YOUNGSTER *CHRISTIAN ERIKSEN* WAS PLAYING AT *ODENSE BOLDKLUB* WHEN HE BEGAN TO ATTRACT THE ATTENTION OF SOME OF THE WORLD'S ELITE TEAMS. HE HAD TRIALS WITH *BARCELONA, CHELSEA, REAL MADRID, MANCHESTER UNITED* AND *AC MILAN* BEFORE OPTING TO JOIN THE YOUTH SET-UP AT *AJAX*. HE BROKE THROUGH AT THE DUTCH GIANTS, WINNING THREE LEAGUE TITLES, THE KNVB CUP AND THE JOHAN CRUYFF SHIELD.

1 WHICH FORMER *SPURS* BOSS WAS HIS MANAGER AT *AJAX?*

2 NAME THE FOUR MANAGERS UNDER WHOM HE PLAYED AT *SPURS* BETWEEN 2013 AND 2020.

3 WHO WAS THE MANAGER WHO SIGNED *ERIKSEN* TO *INTERNAZIONALE* IN 2020?

4 NAME ONE OF THE THREE MANAGERS UNDER WHOM *ERIKSEN* PLAYED WITH THE DANISH NATIONAL TEAM SINCE 2010.

5 *ERIKSEN* WON THE DANISH PLAYER OF THE YEAR AWARD A RECORD FIVE TIMES BETWEEN 2013 AND 2018. WHICH *TOTTENHAM HOTSPUR* PLAYER WON THE AWARD IN 1996?

6 WHICH *TOTTENHAM* PLAYER WON THE DANISH PLAYER OF THE YEAR AWARD IN 2021?

VILLAS-BOAS BOYS

APPOINTED AS **HARRY REDKNAPP'S** SUCCESSOR IN 2012, **ANDRÉ VILLAS-BOAS** STEERED **SPURS** TO THE CLUB'S THEN-RECORD TALLY OF 72 POINTS IN HIS DEBUT SEASON, NARROWLY MISSING OUT ON UEFA CHAMPIONS LEAGUE QUALIFICATION TO **ARSENAL.**

AHEAD OF THE 2012-13 SEASON, HE BROUGHT IN A NUMBER OF PLAYERS -- INCLUDING AMERICAN **CLINT DEMPSEY** FROM **FULHAM** -- BUT TO NO AVAIL, AS HE LEFT THE CLUB BEFORE THE YEAR WAS OUT. IDENTIFY THESE OTHER PLAYERS WHO JOINED **SPURS** DURING THE TENURE OF **ANDRÉ VILLAS-BOAS:**

1 £26 MILLION STRIKER FROM *VALENCIA*, AFTER TWO UNDERWHELMING SEASONS WITH *SPURS* HE RETURNED TO SPAIN WITH *VILLARREAL*.

2 *ARGENTINA* INTERNATIONAL SIGNED FROM *ROMA* FOR £25.8 MILLION PLUS £4.2 MILLION IN ADD-ONS. TOWARDS THE END OF HIS *SPURS* CAREER HE SCORED A SENSATIONAL RABONA IN THE NORTH LONDON DERBY BEFORE GETTING HIMSELF SENT OFF.

3 *BRAZIL* INTERNATIONAL MIDFIELDER WHO HAS PLAYED IN BRAZIL, POLAND, LITHUANIA, ENGLAND, CHINA, SPAIN AND SAUDI ARABIA.

4 *BELGIUM* MIDFIELDER SIGNED FROM *FULHAM* FOR £15 MILLION.

5 *FRANCE* INTERNATIONAL SIGNED FROM *TOULOUSE*, HE SPENT TWO YEARS AT *SPURS* BEFORE JOINING *WATFORD* IN 2015.

6 DANISH STAR SIGNED TO *SPURS* FROM *AJAX*, WITH WHOM HE HAD WON THREE LEAGUE TITLES, HE WON A SERIE A TITLE IN 2021.

7 SIGNED FROM *FC TWENTE*, *BELGIUM* INTERNATIONAL MIDFIELDER WHO SPENT THREE YEARS WITH *TOTTENHAM* BEFORE SIGNING FOR *WEST BROMWICH ALBION*. HE SUBSEQUENTLY MOVED TO *MONACO*, PLAYED AT *ANDERLECHT* ON LOAN AND SIGNED FOR TURKEY'S *İSTANBUL BAŞAKŞEHIR* IN 2020.

8 LEAGUE TITLE WINNER WITH *STEAUA BUCUREŞTI*, ROMANIAN DEFENDER WHO MOVED ON TO *NAPOLI* TWO YEARS AFTER JOINING *TOTTENHAM*.

9 *BELGIUM'S* MOST-CAPPED PLAYER, DEFENDER WHO SPENT EIGHT SEASONS WITH *SPURS* BEFORE JOINING *BENFICA* IN 2020.

10 FORMER *ARSENAL*, *MANCHESTER CITY* AND *REAL MADRID* STRIKER WHOSE LOAN MOVE TO *SPURS* WAS MADE PERMANENT IN 2012. HE JOINED *CRYSTAL PALACE* IN EARLY 2016.

GLENN THE GUVNOR

AS A PLAYER, *GLENN HODDLE* WON TWO FA CUPS AND THE UEFA CUP WITH *SPURS* AND A LEAGUE TITLE WITH *MONACO*, AS WELL AS NUMEROUS INDIVIDUAL HONOURS. HE WAS CAPPED 53 TIMES BY *ENGLAND.*

HE BEGAN HIS MANAGEMENT CAREER AS PLAYER/MANAGER OF *SWINDON TOWN* IN 1991, STEERING THE WILTSHIRE CLUB TO THE PREMIER LEAGUE IN 1993.

1 WHICH FORMER **SPURS** STAR DID **HODDLE** SUCCEED AS MANAGER OF **SWINDON TOWN?**

2 **HODDLE** FOLLOWED WHICH FORMER **CHELSEA** DEFENDER, A EUROPEAN CUP WNNERS' CUP AND FA CUP WINNER AS A PLAYER, AS MANAGER OF **CHELSEA?**

3 WHEN HE TOOK THE **CHELSEA** JOB IN 2003, WHICH FORMER **SPURS** MANAGER DID **HODDLE** APPOINT AS HIS ASSISTANT?

4 WHO DID **HODDLE** REPLACE AS **ENGLAND** MANAGER IN 1996?

5 IN 2000, **GLENN HODDLE** SUCCEEDED **DAVE JONES** AS MANAGER OF WHICH CLUB?

6 **HODDLE** WAS APPOINTED **TOTTENHAM** BOSS IN 2001 FOLLOWING THE SACKING OF WHICH MANAGER?

7 **HODDLE** WAS APPOINTED MANAGER OF WHICH CLUB IN 2004?

TERRY'S WHEELING AND DEALING

BY THE SUMMER OF 1988, IT WAS OBVIOUS THAT **NEWCASTLE UNITED** WOULDN'T BE ABLE TO HOLD ON TO A TALENT LIKE **PAUL GASCOIGNE.** **MANCHESTER UNITED** WERE FAVOURITES TO CAPTURE HIS SIGNATURE AND **GAZZA** ASSURED **ALEX FERGUSON** THAT HE WOULD SIGN FOR **THE RED DEVILS. FERGUSON** DULY WENT ON HOLIDAY TO MALTA -- WHERE HE RECEIVED THE NEWS THAT **GASCOIGNE** HAD SIGNED FOR **SPURS** FOR A RECORD BRITISH FEE OF £2.2 MILLION. **GASCOIGNE** LATER REVEALED THAT HE HAD RECEIVED A £100,000 SIGNING ON FEE, OF WHICH HE SPENT £70,000 BUYING PROPERTY FOR HIS MOTHER AND FATHER.

GASCOIGNE WAS AN ACQUISITION OF WHEELER DEALER BOSS **TERRY VENABLES.** FROM WHICH CLUBS DID **VENABLES** SIGN THESE PLAYERS:

1 STEVE SEDGLEY

2 PAT VAN DEN HAUWE

3 PAUL WALSH

4 BOBBY MIMMS

5 JUSTIN EDINBURGH

6 GUDNI BERGSSON

7 NAYIM

8 JOHN HENDRY

9 MARK ROBSON

10 GARY LINEKER

11 JOHN MONCUR

12 JUSTIN EDINBURGH

13 ERIK THORSTVEDT

14 TERRY FENWICK

GAZZA'S FOLLY

JUST MINUTES INTO THE 1991 FA CUP FINAL BETWEEN *SPURS* AND *NOTTINGHAM FOREST*, AN OVERLY-EAGER *PAUL GASCOIGNE* FOLLOWED AN AGGRESSIVE FOUL ON *GARRY PARKER* WITH A SCYTHING TACKLE ON *GARY CHARLES*. *FOREST* TOOK THE LEAD FROM THE RESULTING FREE-KICK ... AND MOMENTS LATER, *GASCOIGNE* WAS STRETCHERED OFF, HAVING TORN CRUCIATE LIGAMENTS IN THE CHALLENGE. THE INJURY WAS SO SEVERE IT DELAYED HIS IMPENDING MOVE TO ITALY'S *LAZIO* FOR A YEAR!

TOTTENHAM WON THE GAME 2-1 ... BUT WHICH CLUBS DID THE TEAM MEMBERS SUBSEQUENTLY JOIN FROM *SPURS?*

1 JUSTIN EDINBURGH

2 PAT VAN DEN HAUWE

3 STEVE SEDGLEY

4 DAVID HOWELLS

5 PAUL STEWART

6 VINNY SAMWAYS

7 GARY LINEKER

8 PAUL ALLEN

9 PAUL WALSH

10 NAYIM

TEAM MEMBERS *ERIK THORSTVEDT* AND *GARY MABBUTT* RETIRED AFTER PLAYING FOR *SPURS.*

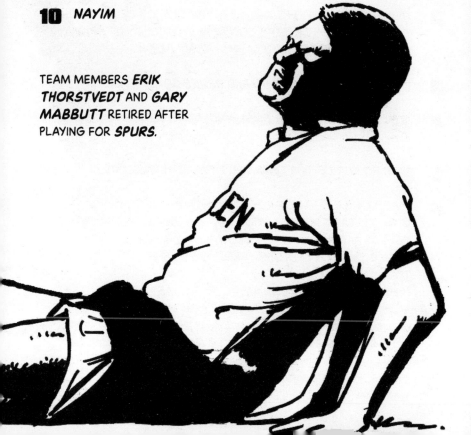

FWA FOOTBALLER OF THE YEAR

FIRST AWARDED TO **STANLEY MATTHEWS** IN 1948, THE FWA FOOTBALLER OF THE YEAR AWARD IS SELECTED BY VOTE OF THE MEMBERS OF THE FOOTBALL WRITERS' ASSOCIATION. **GARETH BALE** WON THE AWARD IN 2013, THE SAME YEAR HE WAS NAMED PREMIER LEAGUE PLAYER OF THE SEASON, PFA YOUNG PLAYER OF THE YEAR, AND WON HIS SECOND PFA PLAYERS' PLAYER OF THE YEAR AWARD.

IDENTIFY THESE OTHER PAST, PRESENT AND FUTURE **TOTTENHAM** PLAYERS WHO WON THE FWA FOOTBALLER OF THE YEAR AWARD.

1 1958: CAPTAIN OF **NORTHERN IRELAND** AND THE **SPURS** TEAM THAT WON THE LEAGUE AND FA CUP DOUBLE THREE YEARS LATER.

2 1969: FORMER **TOTTENHAM HOTSPUR** MIDFIELD GENERAL WHO WAS PLAYING FOR **DERBY COUNTY** WHEN HE SHARED THE AWARD WITH **MANCHESTER CITY** CAPTAIN **TONY BOOK**.

3 1973: **NORTHERN IRELAND** AND **SPURS** GOALKEEPER.

4 1975: **TOTTENHAM** AND **ENGLAND** MIDFIELDER WHO WON THE AWARD DURING HIS SECOND SPELL WITH **FULHAM**.

5 1982: HOLDER OF **TOTTENHAM'S** APPEARANCE RECORD.

6 1986: STRIKER WHO WON BOTH THE PFA PLAYERS' PLAYER OF THE YEAR AND FWA FOOTBALLER OF THE YEAR AWARDS IN THIS DEBUT SEASON AFTER JOINING **EVERTON** FROM **LEICESTER CITY**, HE WOULD JOIN **TOTTENHAM** THREE YEARS LATER.

7 1987: SON OF A **TOTTENHAM** DOUBLE-WINNER, HE SCORED 49 GOALS FOR **SPURS** THE SEASON HE WON THE AWARD.

8 1992: **SPURS** STRIKER WHO WON THE AWARD FOR A SECOND TIME.

9 1993: FORMER **NEWCASTLE UNITED**, **SPURS** AND **MARSEILLE** WINGER WHO WON WHILE PLAYING FOR **SHEFFIELD WEDNESDAY**.

10 1995: GERMAN FORWARD WHO WON IN HIS DEBUT SEASON WITH *SPURS* AFTER JOINING FROM *MONACO*.

11 1999: *FRANCE* WINGER WHO HAD JOINED *TOTTENHAM* FROM *NEWCASTLE UNITED*.

12 2001: FORMER *SPURS* FORWARD WHO WON WHILE PLAYING FOR *MANCHESTER UNITED*, WITH WHOM HE HAD WON THE UEFA CHAMPIONS LEAGUE.

13 2011: *WEST HAM UNITED* MIDFIELDER, HE JOINED *TOTTENHAM* SHORTLY AFTER WINNING THE AWARD.

GOING DUTCH

THE FIRST-EVER RECIPIENT OF THE GOLDEN BOY, THE AWARD GIVEN TO
THE BEST YOUNG PLAYER IN EUROPE'S TOP FLIGHT, *RAFAEL VAN DER
VAART* EARNED THE FIRST OF HIS 109 CAPS FOR THE *NETHERLANDS*
AT THE AGE OF 18. HE JOINED *SPURS* FROM *REAL MADRID* IN 2010 AND
SPENT TWO YEARS AT THE CLUB BEFORE JOINING *HAMBURGER SV*.

FROM WHICH CLUBS WERE THE FOLLOWING DUTCH INTERNATIONALS
SIGNED TO *TOTTENHAM HOTSPUR?*

1 *STEVEN BERGWIJN* -- 2020

2 *VINCENT JANSSEN* -- 2016

3 *MICHEL VORM* -- 2014

4 *EDGAR DAVIDS* -- 2005

5 *JOHN METGOD* -- 1987

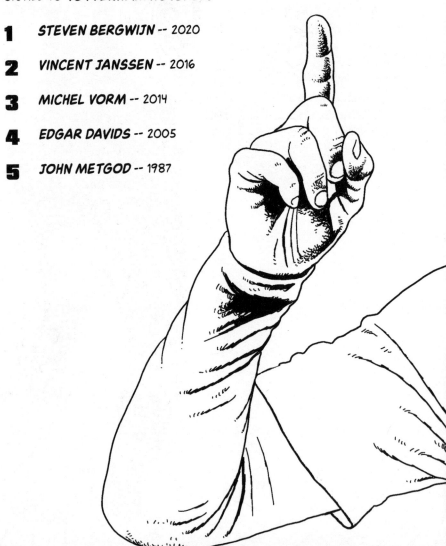

DOWN SOUTH AMERICA WAY

MEMBERS OF THE **ARGENTINA** TEAM THAT WON THE WORLD CUP ON HOME SOIL IN 1978, **RICARDO VILLA** AND **OSSIE ARDILES** WERE SNAPPED UP FOR **TOTTENHAM** BY **KEITH BURKINSHAW**. **RICKY VILLA** WILL FOREVER BE CELEBRATED BY **SPURS** FANS FOR THE WONDER GOAL THAT WON THE 1981 FA CUP FINAL -- A MOMENT SO SPECIAL THAT IT WAS AWARDED THE WEMBLEY GOAL OF THE CENTURY AWARD IN 2001.

FOR WHICH NORTH, SOUTH OR CENTRAL AMERICAN COUNTRIES WERE THE FOLLOWING **TOTTENHAM HOTSPUR** PLAYERS CAPPED:

1 *CRISTIAN ROMERO*

2 *GUSTAVO POYET*

3 *EMERSON ROYAL*

4 *GIOVANI LO CELSO*

5 *CAMERON CARTER-VICKERS*

6 *LUCAS MOURA*

7 *JUAN FOYTH*

8 *WILSON PALACIOS*

9 *DEANDRE YEDLIN*

10 *PAULINHO*

11 *PAULO GAZZANIGA*

12 *SANDRO*

13 *HEURELHO GOMES*

14 *FEDERICO FAZIO*

15 *DAVINSON SÁNCHEZ*

16 *GILBERTO*

17 *GIOVANI DOS SANTOS*

18 *BRAD FRIEDEL*

1001 ANSWERS

Portugeezers! (pg 2)
1. Eric Dier   2. Carlos Vinícius
3. Pedro Mendes
4. José Mourinho
5. Hélder Postiga
6. Jan Vertonghen
7. André Villas-Boas

Greavsie! (pg 4)
1. Chelsea   2. Ron Greenwood
3. A.C. Milan   4. Two
5. Martin Peters   6. London to
Mexico World Cup Rally
7. Barnet   8. Ian St. John
9. "Sporting Triangles"

A Bit of a Knees-Up … (pg 6)
1. Liverpool   2. Luton Town
3. Aston Villa   4. Dundee United
5. Queens Park Rangers
6. West Ham United
7. Newcastle United   8. Huracán
9. Standard de Liège
10. Brighton & Hove Albion

Boro Boys (pg 8)
1. Mido   2. Nick Barmby
3. Kyle Naughton
4. Ryan Fredericks
5. Jonathan Woodgate
6. Cyril Knowles   7. Ugo Ehiogu
8. Terry Venables
9. Paul Gascoigne
10. Luke Young

Maybe it's Because I'm a Londoner (pg 10)
1. George Graham
2. Harry Redknapp
3. Tim Sherwood

4. José Mourinho
5. Glenn Hoddle
6. Jacques Santini
7. Mauricio Pochettino
8. Christian Gross   9. Martin Jol
10. Doug Livermore
11. Osvaldo Ardiles
12. Nuno Espírito Santo
13. David Pleat

FA Cup Kings (pg 12)
1. Osvaldo Ardiles, Steve
Perryman, Chris Hughton,
Glenn Hoddle   2. George Graham
3. Terry Venables
4. Sol Campbell   5. Jimmy
Greaves and Terry Venables
6. Terry Venables   7. Terry
Fenwick   8. Ray Clemence
9. Terry Neill (Arsenal), George
Graham (Arsenal), José Mourinho
(Chelsea), Harry Redknapp
(Portsmouth)
10. The only two player/managers
to win the FA Cup

Le Gardien (pg 14)
1. Moussa Sissoko
2. Étienne Capoue   3. Louis Saha
4. David Ginola   5. William Gallas
6. Tanguy Ndombélé
7. Younès Kaboul

Bravehearts! (pg 16)
1. Dave Mackay   2. John White
3. Alan Gilzean   4. Alan Hutton
5. Colin Calderwood   6. Gordon
Durie   7. Steve Archibald
8. Alan Brazil   9. Neil Sullivan
10. Bill Brown

Crazy Days! (pg 18)
1. Dele Alli   2. Joe Kinnear
3. Adam Smith   4. Andros
Townsend   5. Ben Thatcher
6. Jake Livermore   7. Peter
Shreeves   8. Chris Perry
9. Neil Sullivan   10. John Scales

"Archigoles" (pg 20)
1. Alex Ferguson   2. Keith
Burkinshaw   3. Liverpool
4. Jock Stein, Alex Ferguson
5. Anderlecht   6. Terry Venables
7. Steaua Bucharest   8. Blackburn
Rovers   9. Hibernian, St Mirren,
Clyde, Ayr United, East Fife
10. Fulham   11. Dublin

The Perfect One (pg 22)
1. Middlesbrough
2. Frank Rijkaard   3. Espanyol
4. Martin Jol   5. Gus Poyet
6. Arsenal   7. Jonathan
Woodgate   8. Harry Redknapp
9. Real Madrid
10. Blackburn Rovers

The Boys of '67 (pg 24)
1. Arsenal   2. Brighton & Hove
Albion   3. Fulham   4. Seattle
Sounders   5. Arsenal   6. West
Ham United   7. Highlands Park
8. Queens Park Rangers
9. Southampton   10. Fulham

Them's the Breaks! (pg 26)
1. Dave Mackay   2. Hugo Lloris
3. Terry Medwin   4. Norwich City
5. Son Heung-min
6. Ryan Mason   7. Neil Ruddock

8. Luka Modrić
9. Maurice Norman

Magic Chris (pg 28)
1. Jack Charlton, Arthur Cox
2. Bobby Robson
3. Peter Shreeves, David Pleat,
Terry Venables   4. Red Star
Belgrade   5. Trevor Steven
6. Trevor Francis   7. Arsenal
8. Falkirk, Bradford City,
Sunderland   9. Burnley

The Boys in Green (pg 30)
1. Stephen Carr
2. Andy Reid
3. Stephen Kelly
4. Chris Hughton
5. Gary Doherty   6. Matt Doherty
7. Joe Kinnear   8. Tony Galvin

Harry's Game (pg 32)
1. Leyton Orient, Millwall,
Norwich City, Leicester City
2. Asteras Tripolis
3. Leicester City   4. Lithuania
5. Panama   6. Gary Lineker
7. Bulgaria, Montenegro
8. Emmanuel Adebayor
9. Teddy Sheringham
10. Bobby Smith
11. Michael Owen

Super Pav (pg 34)
1. Jonathan Woodgate
2. Gilberto   3. Alan Hutton
4. Luka Modrić   5. Vedran
Ćorluka   6. Fraizer Campbell

Dive Stations! (pg 36)
1. Nicola Berti   2. Chris Waddle
3. Gordon Durie   4. Nico Claesen
5. Gary Lineker   6. Kasey Keller
7. Richard Gough   8. Chris
Hughton   9. Ilie Dumitrescu

The Prince (pg 38)
1. Martin Jol   2. Harry Redknapp
3. Jürgen Klopp   4. Paul Hart
5. Michael Ballack   6. AC Milan
7. Roberto Di Matteo
8. Eintracht Frankfurt
9. Barcelona   10. Beşiktaş

The Centurions (pg 40)
1. Robbie Keane   2. Clint
Dempsey   3. Pat Jennings
4. Noureddine Naybet
5. Christian Eriksen   6. Rafael van
der Vaart   7. Jürgen Klinsmann
8. Giovani dos Santos   9. Vedran
Ćorluka   10. Kasey Keller

Meet the New Boss, Same as the Old Boss (pg 42)
1. Terry Neill   2. Harry Redknapp
3. Terry Venables   4. Glenn
Hoddle   5. Harry Redknapp
6. Terry Neill   7. Gerry Francis
8. Glenn Hoddle   9. Martin Jol
10. Harry Redknapp

Lilywhite Red Men (pg 44)
1. Neil Ruddock   2. Robbie Keane
3. Ronny Rosenthal
4. Øyvind Leonhardsen

"Musselburgh" (pg 46)
1. Peter Crouch   2. Tim Sherwood
3. Younes Kaboul   4. Dave
Beasant   5. Darren Anderton
6. Sean Davis
7. Teddy Sheringham
8. Niko Kranjčar

The Lane and The Bridge (pg 48)
1. Gustavo Poyet   2. Gordon
Durie   3. Terry Venables
4. Bobby Smith   5. Carlo Cudicini
6. Les Allen   7. Scott Parker
8. Graham Roberts   9. Mark Falco
10. Neil Sullivan

Gazza! (pg 50)
1. Jack Charlton, Willie McFaul
2. Terry Venables   3. Hartlepool
United   4. David Pleat, Terry
Venables, Glenn Hoddle   5. Gary
Charles   6. Dino Zoff   7. Walter
Smith   8. Bryan Robson
9. George Boateng   10. Everton,
Burnley   11. Kettering Town

England Expects (pg 52)
1. Gary Lineker   2. Joe Hart
3. Sol Campbell   4. Martin
Peters   5. Chris Waddle   6. Ray
Clemence   7. Jimmy Greaves
8. Paul Gascoigne   9. Jermain
Defoe   10. Teddy Sheringham
11. Peter Crouch   12. Paul
Robinson   13. Alan Mullery
14. Michael Carrick

Alf's Wingless Wonders (pg 54)
1. Graham Roberts 2. Joe Kinnear 3. Terry Yorath 4. Jürgen Klinsmann 5. Terry Venables 6. Terry Fenwick 7. Mike England 8. Dave Mackay 9. Danny Blanchflower 10. Peter Taylor

The Pitbull (pg 56)
1. Ajax 2. AC Milan 3. Juventus 4. Frank Rijkaard 5. Internazionale 6. Martin Jol 7. Dick Advocaat, Guus Hiddink, Frank Rijkaard, Louis van Gaal, Marco van Basten 8. Crystal Palace 9. Barnet 10. Portugal

The Special One (pg 58)
1. Real Betis 2. PSV Eindhoven 3. PSV Eindhoven 4. Wolverhampton Wanderers 5. Southampton 6. Swansea City 7. Benfica 8. Benfica 9. Real Madrid 10. Burnley

Saintly Boys (pg 60)
1. Victor Wanyama 2. Neil Ruddock 3. Alf Ramsey 4. Kyle Walker-Peters 5. Dean Richards 6. Kasey Keller 7. Jamie Redknapp 8. Frank Saul 9. Paulo Gazzaniga

Gunners Take Charge (pg 62)
1. Dynamo Kyiv 2. Milton Keynes Dons 3. Blackburn Rovers 4. Milton Keynes Dons 5. Liverpool 6. Vitesse Arnhem 7. Luton Town 8. Port Vale

9. Borussia Dortmund 10. Peterborough United 11. Peterborough United 12. East Fife 13. Milton Keynes Dons 14. Le Mans 15. Sheffield Wednesday 16. Sheffield United

Tottenham's World Cup Goalgetters (pg 64)
1. Jimmy Greaves 2. Martin Peters 3. Alan Mullery 4. Darren Anderton 5. Sol Campbell 6. Peter Crouch 7. Jermain Defoe 8. Dele Alli 9. Harry Kane 10. Kieran Trippier

Nice One, Cyril ... (pg 66)
1. Graham Roberts 2. Alan Mullery 3. Chris Hughton 4. Joe Kinnear 5. Terry Yorath 6. Terry Fenwick 7. Gus Poyet

The Willie Hall Haul (pg 68)
1. Jimmy Greaves 2. Teddy Sheringham 3. 1986 4. Gary Lineker 5. Sol Campbell

The Boys of '81 (pg 70)
1. Barnet 2. West Ham United 3. Charlton Athletic 4. Rangers 5. Oxford United 6. Fort Lauderdale Strikers 7. Blackburn Rovers 8. Barcelona 9. Sheffield Wednesday 10. Monaco 11. West Bromwich Albion 12. Norwich City

Keep it Clean! (pg 72)
1. Steve Perryman   2. George Graham   3. Glenn Hoddle
4. Chris Hughton   5. Nuno Espírito Santo   6. Ossie Ardiles

The Midfield Dynamo (pg 74)
1. Lyon   2. Paris Saint-Germain
3. Atlético Madrid
4. Sporting CP   5. Real Madrid
6. Paris Saint-Germain
7. Real Betis   8. Bayer Leverkusen
9. Burnley   10. Ajax   11. Roma
12. Newcastle United   13. Milton Keynes Dons   14. Lyon
15. Real Madrid   16. PSV

The Iceman Cometh (pg 76)
1. Charlton Athletic   2. Newcastle United   3. Southampton
4. Saint-Étienne   5. AJ Auxerre
6. Wigan Athletic   7. Nottingham Forest   8. Hertha BSC
9. Nottingham Forest   10. Roma
11. Lens   12. Benfica
13. Derby County   14. Lens

"The Delstroyer" (pg 78)
1. Olympique Lyon   2. Ajax
3. Newcastle United
4. Bayer 04 Leverkusen
5. Paris Saint-Germain
6. Fulham   7. Paris Saint-Germain
8. AZ Alkmaar
9. Atlético de Madrid
10. Real Betis   11. Swansea City
12. Southampton   13. Olympique Lyon   14. Marseille
15. Swansea City   16. Estudiantes
17. Leeds United   18. Sevilla
19. 1. FC Köln   20. Montpellier
21. Swansea City   22. Sporting CP
23. Burnley   24. Seattle Sounders

Ossie! Ossie! Ossie! (pg 80)
1. Blackburn Rovers   2. Queens Park Rangers   3. Swindon Town
4. Newcastle United
5. West Bromwich Albion
6. Tottenham Hotspur

The Old Firm (pg 82)
1. Cameron Carter-Vickers
2. Ramon Vega   3. Alfie Conn Jr.
4. Niko Kranjčar   5. John Gorman
6. Jermain Defoe   7. Victor Wanyama   8. Paul Gascoigne
9. Graham Roberts
10. Robbie Keane

From North London to the Far East (pg 84)
1. Gary Lineker   2. Mousa Dembélé   3. Carl Hoddle
4. Paul Gascoigne   5. Eiður Guðjohnsen   6. Frédéric Kanouté

Yankee Doodle Dempsey (pg 86)
1. Michael Brown   2. Scott Parker
3. Steed Malbranque
4. Ryan Sessegnon
5. Terry Dyson   6. Alan Mullery

Semi-Skinned (pg 88)
1. Preston North End
2. Blackpool   3. Manchester City
4. Standard Liège   5. Arsenal
6. Chelsea   7. Liverpool
8. Newcastle United   9. Barcelona
10. Arsenal   11. Nottingham Forest   12. Arsenal   13. Everton

14. Newcastle United   15. Arsenal
16. Arsenal   17. Portsmouth
18. Chelsea   19. Chelsea
20. Manchester United
21. Chelsea

Madridistas (pg 90)
1. Roberto Soldado   2. Rafael van der Vaart   3. Luka Modrić
4. Sergio Reguilón
5. Gareth Bale   6. José Mourinho
7. César Sánchez   8. Jonathan Woodgate   9. Juande Ramos

Charity Begins at Home (pg 92)
1. Newcastle United   2. Les Allen
3. Ipswich Town   4. Goalkeeper Pat Jennings scored with an upfield punt that bounced over United's goalkeeper Alex Stepney
5. Mark Falco   6. Liverpool
7. Arsenal

Carling Darlings (pg 94)
1. Blackburn Rovers
2. Aston Villa   3. Stoke City
4. Sunderland   5. Everton
6. Queens Park Rangers
7. Sevilla   8. Sunderland
9. Liverpool   10. Manchester United   11. Queens Park Rangers
12. Portsmouth   13. Sunderland
14. Hull City   15. Sunderland

Gone Too Soon? (pg 96)
1. William Gallas   2 Laurie Brown
3. Rohan Ricketts
4. Sol Campbell   5. David Jenkins
6. Willie Young

Africa! Afrique! (pg 98)
1. Kenya   2. Togo   3. Ghana
4. Mali   5. Morocco   6. Cameroon
7. South Africa   8. Algeria
9. Ivory Coast   10. Nigeria
11. Cameroon   12. Morocco
13. Algeria   14. South Africa
15. Ivory Coast   16. Morocco

Big Chiv (pg 100)
1. Ralph Coates   2. Steve Archibald   3. Allan Nielsen
4. Christian Ziege   5. Dimitar Berbatov, Jonathan Woodgate

The Fortunate Son (pg 102)
1. Toby Alderweireld and Jan Vertonghen   2. Stephen Carr
3. Simon Davies   4. Erik Thorstvedt   5. Neil Sullivan

The Handsome One (pg 104)
1. Newcastle United   2. Crystal Palace   3. Newcastle United
4. Rosenborg BK   5. Liverpool
6. Sporting CP   7. Bröndby
8. Sheffield Wednesday
9. Queens Park Rangers
10. Charlton Athletic   11. Cagliari

The Real Mackay (pg 106)
1. John Chiedozie   2. Hossam Ghaly   3. Tom Huddlestone
4. Grzegorz Rasiak

Imported From Porto (pg 108)
1. Southampton 2. Leeds United
3. Liverpool 4. Red Star Belgrade
5. West Ham United 6. Chelsea
7. Brighton & Hove Albion
8. Red Star Belgrade
9. Excelsior Mouscron
10. Manchester United
11. Liverpool 12. Rayo Vallecano
13. Arsenal 14. Charlton Athletic
15. Portsmouth 16. Shimizu
S-Pulse 17. Internazionale

Totally Hammered! (pg 110)
1. Mauricio Taricco
2. Jimmy Greaves
3. Michael Carrick
4. Scott Parker
5. Frédéric Kanouté
6. Bobby Zamora
7. Les Ferdinand

Bouncing Straight Back (pg 112)
1. Watford 2. St. George
3. Bulova SA 4. Derby County
5. Vancouver Whitecaps
6. Manchester City 7. Chelsea
8. Charlton Athletic 9. Bolton
Wanderers 10. Leyton Orient
11. Charlton Athletic 12. Coventry
City 13. Oxford United
14. Portland Timbers
15. Charlton Athletic
16. Southend United
17. Leyton Orient
18. Tampa Bay Rowdies

Players of the Year (pg 114)
1. Dimitar Berbatov 2. David
Ginola 3. Luka Modrić
4. Jürgen Klinsmann

5. Vlad Chicheș
6. Clint Dempsey, Brad Friedel,
Kasey Keller 7. Jan Vertonghen

Ever-Present Perryman (pg 116)
1. Gary Mabbutt 2. Pat Jennings
3. Tom Morris 4. Cyril Knowles
5. Glenn Hoddle
6. Ted Ditchburn 7. Alan Gilzean
8. Jimmy Dimmock 9. Phil Beal

The Italian Job (pg 118)
1. Lazio 2. Internazionale
3. Avellino 4. Sampdoria
5. Vicenza 6. Juventus
7. Napoli 8. Napoli 9. Genoa
10. Roma 11. Internazionale
12. Internazionale 13. AC Milan
14. Roma

Monikers! (pg 120)
1. Gus Poyet 2. Marc Falco
3. Erik Thorstvedt 4. Clint
Dempsey 5. Steve Sedgley
6. Gary Doherty 7. Gordon Durie
8. Christian Eriksen 9. Danny
Rose 10. Ronny Rosenthal
11. Maurice Norman 12. Tony
Galvin 13. Mauricio Taricco
14. Terry Naylor 15. Matthew
Etherington 16. Lee Young-pyo
17. Paul Robinson 18. Benoît
Assou-Ekotto 19. Erik Lamela
20. Neil Ruddock

G-Man Gillie (pg 122)
1. Mbulelo Mabizela 2. Peter Baker 3. Richard Gough 4. Alan Mullery 5. Steven Pienaar 6. Pat van den Hauwe 7. Danny Blanchflower 8. Ally Dick

The Numbers Game (pg 124)
1. Heung-min Son 2. Robbie Keane 3. Luka Modrić 4. Dele Alli 5. Jermain Defoe 6. Lucas Moura 7. Peter Crouch 8. Giovani dos Santos 9. Mousa Dembélé

"Loser Takes Ball" (pg 126)
1. Southampton: George Burley; Tottenham: Martin Jol, Juande Ramos, Harry Redknapp, André Villas-Boas, José Mourinho, Ryan Mason; Real Madrid: Julen Lopetegui, Santiago Solari, Zinédine Zidane, Rafael Benítez, Carlo Ancelotti 2. John Toshack, Brian Flynn, Gary Speed, Chris Coleman, Ryan Giggs, Robert Page

Oh, Danny Boy ... (pg 128)
1. Northampton Town 2. Durban United 3. Derby County 4. Fulham 5. Brighton & Hove Albion 6. Queens Park Rangers 7. Fulham 8. Southampton

The Boys of '84 (pg 130)
1. Brentford 2. Rangers 3. Charlton Athletic 4. West Ham United 5. Portsmouth 6. Oxford United 7. Chelsea

8. Sheffield Wednesday 9. Watford 10. West Bromwich Albion 11. Bournemouth 12. Norwich City 13. Blackburn Rovers 14. Norwich City 15. Ajax

Coming to America ... and Canada, too! (pg 132)
1. Mike England 2. New England Revolution, Seattle Sounders 3. Brad Friedel 4. LA Galaxy 5. Thierry Henry 6. Lee Young-pyo 7. Jermain Defoe 8. DeAndre Yedlin 9. Richard Gough 10. Kasey Keller

Comings and Goings (pg 134)
1. Villarreal 2. Al-Duhail SC 3. Watford 4. Celtic 5. Watford 6. Fulham 7. Sevilla 8. Metz 9. Degerfors 10. Celtic 11. Real Madrid 12. Benfica

Record Breakers! (pg 136)
1. Tanguy Ndombele 2. Alfie Devine 3. Brad Friedel 4. Crewe Alexandra 5. Steve Perryman 6. Bayer Leverkusen 7. Pat Jennings 8. Jermain Defoe 9. 1. FC Köln 10. Wigan Athletic

Record Makers! (pg 138)

1. "Diamond Lights"   2. "Ossie's Dream (Spurs Are on Their Way to Wembley)"   3. "Glory, Glory, Tottenham Hotspur"
4. "Tottenham, Tottenham"
5. Steve Archibald
6. "Hot Shot Tottenham"
7. Lindisfarne
8. "When The Year Ends in One"
9. Basile Boli

The Boy From Beckton (pg 140)

1. Bournemouth   2. Portsmouth
3. Tottenham Hotspur
4. Sunderland   5. Toronto FC
6. Sunderland   7. Rangers
8. West Ham United
9. Sunderland
10. Tottenham Hotspur

A Royal Title (pg 142)

1. Paulinho   2. Mido   3. Nayim

Dragon's Men (pg 144)

1. Ben Davies   2. Mel Hopkins
3. Terry Yorath   4. Mike England
5. Pat van den Hauwe
6. Joe Rodon   7. Mark Bowen
8. Simon Davies   9. Chris Gunter

Spurs Celebs! (pg 146)

1. Jude Law   2. Marina Sirtis
3. Salma Rushdie   4. Dave Clark
5. Trevor McDonald
6. J.K. Rowling
7. Kenneth Branagh
8. Leslie Phillips
9. Adele   10. Jah Wobble
11. Michael McIntyre
12. Roger Lloyd-Pack
13. Rupert Grint

The Hod Squads (pg 148)

1. Gerry Francis   2. David Pleat
3. Terry Neill   4. Keith Burkinshaw
5. Harry Redknapp   6. Peter Shreeves   7. Jacques Santini
8. Mauricio Pochettino   9. Terry Venables   10. Christian Gross
11. Juande Ramos

Sevilla Service (pg 150)

1. Didier Zokora   2. Frédéric Kanouté   3. Erik Lamela
4. Federico Fazio
5. Ilie Dumitrescu

The Ghost of White Hart Lane (pg 152)

1. Dave Mackay   2. Graeme Souness   3. Bill Brown
4. George Graham
5. Alan Gilzean
6. Steve Archibald
7. Richard Gough   8. Joe Jordan

The Goals That Brought The Glory! (pg 154)

1. Sandy Brown (2)
2. John Cameron, Tom Smith, Sandy Brown
3. Jimmy Dimmock
4. Bobby Smith, Terry Dyson
5. Jimmy Greaves, Bobby Smith, Danny Blanchflower
6. Jimmy Robertson, Frank Saul
7. Tommy Hutchison (o.g.)
8. Ricardo Villa (2), Garth Crooks
9. Clive Allen, Gary Mabbutt

10. Paul Stewart,
Des Walker (o.g.)

Show Me the Money! (pg 156)
1. Kyle Walker 2. Michael Carrick
3. Kevin Wimmer 4. Robbie
Keane 5. Nabil Bentaleb
6. Gareth Bale 7. Kieran Trippier
8. Christian Eriksen

"Second is Nothing" (pg 158)
1. Liverpool 2. Manchester
United 3. Manchester United
4. Everton 5. Feyenoord
6. Liverpool 7. Coventry City
8. Blackburn Rovers
9. Manchester United 10. Chelsea
11. Chelsea 12. Liverpool
13. Manchester City

Not the Face! Not the Face! (pg 160)
1. Gary Mabbutt 2. Michael
Dawson 3. Goran Bunjevčević
4. Vlad Chiricheş 5. Mel Hopkins
6. Graham Roberts 7. Harry Kane
8. Jan Vertonghen 9. Milija
Aleksic 10. Kieran Trippier

"Dillinger" (pg 162)
1. Argentina 2. Netherlands
3. Scotland 4. Czech Republic
5. Norway 6. Norway 7. Brazil
8. Canada 9. Spain 10. Norway

The Boys of '72 (pg 164)
1. Arsenal 2. Brighton and Hove
Albion 3. Fulham 4. Seattle
Sounders 5. Brighton & Hove
Albion 6. Highlands Park

7. Oxford United 8. Servette
9. Norwich City 10. St George
11. Millwall 12. Bulova SA
13. Charlton Athletic
14. Portland Timbers

"El Tel" (pg 166)
1. Gheorghe Popescu
2. Giovani dos Santos 3. Nayim
4. Edgar Davids 5. Emerson
Royal 6. Eiður Guðjohnsen
7. Kevin-Prince Boateng
8. Gary Lineker

The Boys of '63 (pg 168)
1. Dundee 2. Enfield
3. Norwich City 4. Aston Villa
5. Torino 6. Falkirk 7. Swansea
Town 8. A.C. Milan 9. Chelsea
10. Scarborough

The Honduran (pg 170)
1. Birmingham City
2. Wigan Athletic
3. Peter Crouch
4. Miami FC

Poachers Turned Gamekeepers (pg 172)
1. Terry Neill 2. David Pleat
3. Jacques Santini
4. Mauricio Pochettino
5. Gerry Francis
6. Keith Burkinshaw

Threepeats! (pg 174)

1. Portsmouth 2. Wigan Athletic
3. Portsmouth 4. Real Madrid
5. Internacional
6. Newcastle United
7. Sheffield United
8. Sheffield United
9. Portsmouth
10. West Ham United 11. Everton
12. Sunderland 13. Portsmouth
14. Manchester City 15. Juventus

Mr. Tottenham Hotspur (pg 176)

1. John Cameron
2. Peter McWilliam
3. Keith Burkinshaw
4. Keith Burkinshaw
5. Keith Burkinshaw
6. David Pleat
7. Terry Venables
8. George Graham
9. Glenn Hoddle
10. Juande Ramos
11. Harry Redknapp
12. Mauricio Pochettino
13. Ryan Mason

Hot Shots! (pg 178)

1. Steffen Iversen 2. Gareth Bale
3. John Duncan 4. Bobby Smith
5. Gus Poyet 6. Darren Bent
7. Clive Allen

Party Like It's 1999 (pg 180)

1. Leicester City 2. Newcastle
United 3. Arsenal 4. Watford
5. Portsmouth 6. Birmingham
City 7. 1. FC Kaiserslautern
8. Watford 9. West Ham United
10. Wolverhampton Wanderers
11. Watford 12. Charlton Athletic

13. 1. FC Kaiserslautern
14. Wolverhampton Wanderers
15. Bolton Wanderers

Well, I Never ... (pg 182)

1. Terry Venables 2. Scott Parker
3. Cyril Knowles (brother of Peter
Knowles) 4. Bill Nicholson
5. "Escape to Victory"
6. Pat van den Hauwe
7. David Ginola

The Creative Croatian (pg 184)

1. Niko Kranjčar 2. Juande Ramos
3. José Mourinho 4. Slaven Bilić
5. Hugo Lloris

Hat-Trick Heroes (pg 186)

1. Jermain Defoe 2. Willie Hall
3. Alfie Stokes 4. Crewe
Alexandra 5. Lucas Moura
6. Son Heung-Min, Harry Kane

The Christian way (pg 188)

1. Martin Jol 2. Tim Sherwood,
André Villas-Boas, Mauricio
Pochettino, José Mourinho
3. Antonio Conte 4. Morten
Olsen, Åge Hareide, Kasper
Hjulmand 5. Allan Nielsen
6. Pierre-Emile Højbjerg

Villas-Boas Boys (pg 190)

1. Robert Soldado 2. Erik Lamela
3. Paulinho 4. Mousa Dembélé
5. Étienne Capoue
6. Christian Eriksen
7. Nacer Chadli 8. Vlad Chiriches
9. Jan Vertonghen
10. Emmanuel Adebayor

Glenn the Guvnor (pg 192)
1. Ossie Ardiles 2. David Webb
3. Peter Shreeves
4. Terry Venables
5. Southampton
6. George Graham
7. Wolverhampton Wanderers

Terry's Wheeling and Dealing (pg 194)
1. Coventry City 2. Everton
3. Liverpool 4. Everton
5. Southend United
6. Valur Reykjavík 7. Barcelona
8. Dundee 9. Watford
10. Barcelona 11. Brentford
12. Southend United
13. IFK Göteborg
14. Queens Park Rangers

Gazza's Folly (pg 196)
1. Portsmouth 2. Millwall
3. Ipswich Town 4. Southampton
5. Liverpool 6. Everton
7. Nagoya Grampus
8. Southampton 9. Portsmouth
10. Zaragoza

FWA Footballer of the Year (pg 198)
1. Danny Blanchflower
2. Dave Mackay 3. Pat Jennings
4. Alan Mullery
5. Steve Perryman
6. Gary Lineker 7. Clive Allen
8. Gary Lineker 9. Chris Waddle
10. Jürgen Klinsmann
11. David Ginola
12. Teddy Sheringham
13. Scott Parker

Going Dutch (pg 200)
1. PSV 2. AZ Alkmaar
3. Swansea City 4. Internazionale
5. Nottingham Forest

Down South America Way (pg 202)
1. Argentina 2. Uruguay
3. Brazil 4. Argentina
5. USA 6. Brazil 7. Argentina
8. Honduras 9. USA 10. Brazil
11. Argentina 12. Brazil 13. Brazil
14. Argentina 15. Colombia
16. Brazil 17. Mexico 18. USA

TRIVQUIZ

FROM ABBA TO ZAPPA, AMÉLIE TO ZULU, AND AGÜERO TO ZIDANE

NEW FOOTBALL AND POP CULTURE QUIZZES
EVERY DAY AT TRIVQUIZ.COM

 trivquiz.com trivquiz trivquiz trivquizcomic